D1608189

KOSTYA

GRAND DUKE KONSTANTIN KONSTANTINOVICH

Compiled and Edited
by Paul Gilbert

Independently Published
by Paul Gilbert
- 2022 -

Published by Paul Gilbert
Independent Researcher

Copyright © 2022

E-mail:
royalrussia@yahoo.com

Blog:
tsarnicholas.org

All rights reserved under international copyright conventions. No part of this book may be reproduced or utilized in any manner in any form or by any means, whatsoever, including electronic or mechanical, including photocopying, scanning, recording, or by any information storage and retrieval system, without written permission except in the case of brief quotations embodied in critical articles and reviews.

This book is sold subject to the condition that it shall not, by way of trade or otherwise, be lent, resold, hired out, or otherwise circulated without the publisher's prior consent in any form of binding or cover other than in which it is published and without a similar condition including this condition imposed on the subsequent purchaser.

ISBN: 9798437181072

TABLE OF CONTENTS

Equestrian portrait of Grand Duke Konstantin Konstantinovich. Early 1900s. Artist: Victor Vikentievich Mazurovsky (1859-1944). From the Collection of the State Historical Museum, Moscow

INTRODUCTION

by Paul Gilbert

This is the first English language publication, dedicated to one of the most beloved and highly respected members of the Romanov dynasty: Grand Duke Konstantin Konstantinovich (1858-1915).

The fourth child of Grand Duke Konstantin Nikolaevich (1827-1892) and his wife Grand Duchess Alexandra Iosifovna (1830-1911), born Princess Alexandra of Saxe-Altenburg, Grand Duke Konstantin was born on 23rd August [O.S. 10 August] 1858 at the Konstantin Palace, in Strelna.

From his early childhood Konstantin was more interested in letters, art, and music than in the military upbringing required for other grand dukes. During his life, he became a poet and playwright of some renown, writing under the pen name "K.R.", the initials of his given name and family name, Konstantin Romanov.

Within the Russian Imperial Family, he was nicknamed 'Kostya'.

Grand Duke Konstantin and his wife Grand Duchess Elizaveta Mavrikievna were among the relatively few Romanovs on intimate terms with Emperor Nicholas II[1] and Empress Alexandra

Feodorovna, who found Konstanin's devotion to his family a welcome respite from the playboy life-style of many of the other grand dukes. In addition, the Grand Duke's artistic slavophilism[2] and devotion to duty endeared him to the Emperor.

He owned numerous residences, including the Marble Palace and an apartment building (Spasskaya st., 21) in St. Petersburg, a palace in Pavlovsk, and the Ostashevo estate in Mozhaisk and Ruzsky districts, near Moscow. In addition, he owned vast plots of land, including part of the Uch-Dere estate in the Sochi district of the Black Sea province, plots of land in the area of the Kherati and Kudebti rivers in the Black Sea province (1287 acres, together with his brother Dmitri), two separate plots from the Mir state forest dacha of the Serpukhov forestry of the Podolsky district of the Moscow province.

In 1884, Konstantin married his second cousin Princess Elisabeth of Saxe-Altenburg (1865-1927), in St. Petersburg. Upon her marriage, Elisabeth became the Grand Duchess Elizabeth Mavrikievna[3]. She was known within the family as "Mavra." Konstantin was, by all accounts, devoted to his wife and children, and a loving father.

The couple had a total of nine children. Their children were the first to fall under the new Family Law promulgated by Emperor Alexander III. It stated that henceforth, only the children and male-line grandchildren of a Tsar would be styled Grand Duke or Grand Duchess with the style of Imperial Highness, whereas the great-grandchildren and their descendants would be styled either "Prince" or "Princess" of the Imperial Blood" with the style of Highness. The revised Family Law was intended to cut down on the number of persons entitled to salaries from the Imperial Treasury. Their children:

1. Prince Ioann (1886–1918)
2. Prince Gabriel (1887–1955)
3. Princess Tatiana (1890–1979)
4. Prince Konstantin (1891–1918)
5. Prince Oleg (1892–1914)
6. Prince Igor (1894–1918)
7. Prince Georgy (1903–1938)
8. Princess Natalia (died at two months, 1905)
9. Princess Vera (1906–2001)

A secret life and a tormented soul

Despite Konstantin's devotion to his wife, the deeply religious grand duke lived a secret life, one which tormented him. As exemplary and dedicated (and even conservative) as his public life was, his private internal turmoil was intense. Had it not been for the publication of his strikingly candid diaries long after his death[4], the world would have never known that this most prolific of the Romanov Grand Dukes, the father of nine children, was tormented by homosexual feelings.

His first homosexual experiences occurred in the Imperial Guards. Konstantin made great efforts to repress his feelings. But despite his love for his wife, he could not resist the temptations offered to a person of his exalted state. Konstantin claimed in his diary that between 1893 and 1899 he remained away from the practice of what he referred to as his "main sin." Yet by the birth of his seventh child George, he had become a regular visitor to several of the bath houses of St. Petersburg.

The cycle of resistance and capitulation to temptation is a common theme of his diaries:

19th September 1902: "How happy I was to free my conscience from the heavy burden of sin, which I accumulated during my trip down the Volga, when instead of thanking God for my recovery, I wilfully transgressed. I have again firmly resolved to liberate myself from my main sin."

19th November 1903: [I have been called] 'the best man in Russia'. But I know what this 'best man' is really like. How appalled all those people, who love and respect me, would be if they knew of my depravity! I am deeply dissatisfied with myself."

24th November 1903: "I again feel a surge of renewed strength and am ready to do battle with my passions. It's always like this after I have fallen; but this time I think I have more determination than I did for instance 10 years ago."

15th December 1903: "I have been reading through my diaries for the past 10 and 20 years. I am not pleased with myself. Ten years ago, I started out on the right path, I began to struggle earnestly with my main vice, and did not sin for seven years, or more correctly, only sinned in my thoughts. In 1900, already after my appointment as head of the military training institutions, I went astray during the summer in Strelna.

"Then it was better for two years, but in 1902, after my illness, I sinned a lot during my trip on the Volga. Finally this year, 1903, I have gone completely astray and have lived in a constant state of war with my conscience.

"The trip to Moscow and Tver seemed to have distracted me from unclean thoughts and desires, but now they have taken me over again. I keep struggling, telling myself that God has given me the heart, intellect and strength to fight successfully.

"The misfortune is that even though I could fight, I don't want to, I weaken, forget my fear of God and fall; I know that the longer it goes on, the more ingrained the habit becomes and the more difficult and painful is the struggle. I almost gave in again, but this time resisted. But for how long? Help me, Lord! The Lord may help, but I myself reject his aid."

28th December 1903: "My life flows on happily, I am truly 'favoured by fate', I am loved, respected, appreciated, I am lucky and successful

Pavlovsk Palace

The Konstantin Palace at Strelna

The Marble Palace in St. Petersburg

Ostashevo, the country estate of Grand Duke Konstantin
Konstantinovich, situated outside of Moscow

in everything that I do, but I lack the one essential thing: inner peace.

"I am completely possessed by my secret vice. For quite a long time, I had almost succeeded in overcoming it, from the end of 1893 until 1900. But since then, and particularly since April of this year (just before the birth of our delightful Georgy) I again slipped up and started to roll as if down an incline, lower and lower all the time.

"And yet I, who stand in charge of the education of a large number of children and youths, should be well acquainted with the standards of morality.

"Finally, I am no longer young, I am married, I have 7 children and old age is not so far away. But I am just like a weather-vane: sometimes I make a firm resolution, I pray devoutly, I stand for the whole of the service immersed in fervent prayers, and yet—immediately afterwards, with the return of impure thoughts everything is forgotten, and I surrender to the power of sin.

"Is the change for the better really so unrealizable? Must I continue wallowing in sin?"

9th January 1904: "For two weeks I have been in harmony with my conscience. It is always like this after I have sinned. At first after transgressing, the sin seems revolting, the heart is full of contrition and repentance, the imagination is clear and impure thoughts no longer invade the mind.

"But as time passes, the depraved passion, at first unnoticeable and barely smouldering, gradually flares up into a conflagration, which envelopes the mind and soul; seductive thoughts become more invasive, I cannot pray, and feel that I am sinking deeper and lower into the mire of vice.

"At the moment for instance, after two weeks in a clear and pious mood, that which I thought I could resist has begun to acquire a seductive charm. Now is the time to be on guard, and to control the imagination, not letting it become a prey to impure thoughts. Will the Lord not help me in my struggle?

"Of course He will help me, I am deeply convinced of this. But my mind has been spoilt, I cannot direct my thoughts as I wish, and give in to my vice almost without resisting. It has been thus since the spring, and all summer and autumn of this last year. And yet before, there were those happy years, when I emerged victorious from the struggle. How to repeat those blessed years from 1893 to 1899?"

20th January 1904: "I lived in peace with my conscience from 27th December, but for the last few days seductive thoughts keep coming into my mind.

"As I was coming home, I ordered my coachmen to turn right along the Moika channel; before reaching the Nevsky I got out, let Foma [coachman] go, and continued on foot past the bath-house.

"I intended to walk straight on—there were some people who recognized me by the door to the bath-house. But without reaching the Pevchesky bridge, I turned back and went in. I took a cubicle.

"And so I have surrendered again, without much struggle, to my depraved inclinations; I have again become inexpressibly disgusting and revolting to myself. Will I never be free of this?"

14th November 1904: "I am fasting, trying to attain the remission of my sins, or rather of my main, mortal sin, and hope that I will be successful.

"It torments me to think that I: sin, I become worse the whole time, I deserve God's wrath, but instead only receive God's favours. My sin is known to no one, I am loved, praised and promoted beyond what I deserve, my life is happy, I have a beautiful wife, who is appreciated and respected by all; delightful children; and finally I have received a special mark of favour from the throne—a mandate recognizing my services; a girl's gymnasium has been named after me. How is it I can't deal with it?

23rd March 1904: "My spiritual state is bad. From the day of my departure from Nizhny [Novgorod], on the 11th, I have been overwhelmed with impure thoughts, which unceasingly pursue me with enticing scenes, compiled by my depraved imagination from former memories.

"I nearly succumbed to temptation in Moscow, but by some happy occurrence I was able to be firm and resist. Even now I am not at peace with my conscience, I try to bargain and—oh horror!—say to myself that once Easter is over, I will be able to give into sin again.

19th April 1904: "My mind is in a bad way again pursued by sinful thoughts, recollections and desires. I dream of going along to the bath-house on the Moika or to have the baths heated up at home, I can picture the familiar attendants, Alexei, Frolov and particularly Sergei Syroezkin. My predilection has always been for simple men; I have never sought, nor found, partners in sin outside their circle. When passion speaks, the arguments of conscience, virtue and reason are silenced."

15th May 1904: "As a result of recollecting former years, I have one again fallen under the influence of impure thoughts, entering dreams and imaginings. My way lay past the baths. I was sure that if I saw one of the attendants at the doors—I would not be able to resist and would go in. I was extremely agitated, all thoughts of virtue were stifled, I had almost lost the capacity of thinking sanely, and was ready to give in to temptation without much struggle. The doors to the bath-house were open, but there were no attendants in sight. By some miracle I refrained and drove past.

"Now, you would think that this victory over

myself would be a cause of joy, but no, quite the contrary, I was furious with myself for a long while afterwards, for not making the most of a convenient opportunity and going in."

21st May 1904: "I was overwhelmed by sinful thoughts during the committee meeting. I dismissed my coachman on the Morskaya, before reaching the corner with the Nevsky, and continued on foot.

"I walked up and down twice past the bathhouse doors; on the third time, I went in. And so, I have once again sinned in the same way. My mood is absolutely foul."

17th June 1904: "In the morning, I used the baths at home. And so failed once more to keep up the fight."

23rd June 1904: "I again renounced the struggle with my desires; it's not that I couldn't, I just didn't want to fight. In the evening they heated up our bath-house for me. The attendant Sergei Syroezkin was busy, so he brought along his brother, twenty-year-old Kondraty, who works as an attendant in the Usachevikh baths.

"And I led the lad astray. Perhaps I caused him to sin for the first time, but it was already too late when I remembered the awesome words: Woe to him who leads even one of these young astray."

26th July 1904: "In the morning, the bathhouse. And once again I find myself, like a squirrel on a wheel, in exactly the same place."

In the autumn of 1904, Konstantin became

somewhat attached to an attractive young man by the name of Yatsko.

12th September 1904: "I sent for Yatsko and he came to see me this morning. I easily persuaded him to be candid. It was strange for me to hear him describe the familiar characteristics: he has never felt drawn to a woman, and has been infatuated with men several times. I did not confess to him that I knew these feelings from my own personal experience. Yatsko and I talked for a long time.

"Before leaving he kissed my face and hands; I should not have allowed this, and should have pushed him away, however I was punished afterwards by vague feelings of shame and remorse. He told me that, ever since the first time we met, his soul has been filled with rapturous feelings towards me, which grow all the time. How this reminds me of my own youth."

A few days later, Konstantin and Yatsko met again, and a relationship developed between the two.

15th September 1904: "I returned by the road along which Yatsko would come in the carriage sent to fetch him. I called for him in order to fulfil his wish to visit me once more and say goodbye before his departure for Vilnius. I admit I was looking forward to seeing him, while at the same time dreading another meeting.

"Now I know that his tendencies are the same as mine, I must be wary. Last time, I re-

The most august poet forever leaves his beloved Pavlovsk.
Page from the Russian magazine «Огонёк»

The funeral procession makes its way through the streets of
Petrograd on 8th June (O.S.) 1915. Emperor Nicholas II can
be seen walking behind the funeral carriage.

strained myself, but who can guarantee the future. He confessed his sins to me with even greater candour; he feels depressed, disgusted with himself, and suffers from pangs of conscience. I tried to cheer him up, certainly I did not reject him and I think I made him feel better, telling him that one has to forget the past and start to live afresh. And he was afraid that I might despise him.

"He told me the names of people who I had vaguely suspected of unnatural tendencies; Yatsko has sinned with several of them, but has now, it seems, firmly decided to give it all up. May God help him."

28th December 1904: "I was plagued all day by bad thoughts. In the evening I felt like going to the bath-house, but for some reason did not. Now it is nearly 11 o'clock. Why didn't I go?

"I am afraid of sin, afraid of going against my conscience, and yet I still want to sin. This struggle is exhausting."

29th December 1904: "Yet another day spoiled by bad thoughts. It must be physiological; it can't just be a question of decadence and lack of will. Some days when these thoughts occur, it is easy to banish them; at other times I am totally besieged by them. I mustn't give in, I must bear it until I feel better again.

"So, I have resisted for another day. But I don't feel like praying."

30th December 1904: "The bad thoughts

hounded me less today. Conscience and reason tell me I should forsake the path of indulgence once and for all, that is to say no longer go to the bath-house, either at home or outside.

"But my feelings and my will rebel—I want to see Sergei Syroezkin, whom I should not lead into temptation, since he is the first to wish it. That is the struggle. Lord help me.

"Will I free myself from sin, will I conquer myself, or will sin overcome me? What will the new year bring us?"

In his final years, he wrote of his homosexual urges less and less, whether from having reached some arrangement with his conscience, or from the natural advance of age and ill health.

A broken heart

The first year of the First World War took a cruel toll on Konstantin's immediate family. Five of his six sons served in the Russian Army, and in October 1914, his fourth and most talented son, Prince of the Imperial Blood Oleg Konstantinovich, was mortally wounded fighting against the Germans. The following Spring, his son-in-law Prince Bagration-Muhransky[5] was killed in battle on the Caucasus front.

Konstantin's health and spirit were broken by these blows, he died on 15th June (O.S. 2nd June) 1915 in his study in Pavlovsk, in the presence of his nine-year-old daughter Vera.

On 2nd June, Nicholas II wrote in his diary: "After the report, little Georgy Konstantinovich came in and announced the death of Kostya. At 9.15 we went to Pavlovsk for the first requiem service. Aunt Olga[6], Mavra and Mitya were present; none of his grown-up sons were there. Returned home at 10.45".

On 8th June, he made another sad entry: "At 10.30, I set out with Ella, Olga, Tatiana and Maria to town, straight to the Peter and Paul Cathedral. The requiem service and funeral lasted two and a half hours. It was sad to look at Aunt Olga, Mavra, and particularly poor Tatiana Konstantinovna, when they lowered Kostya's body into the grave!"

Konstantin's death "was a great loss both for the Sovereign and for the entire Imperial Family, who lost in the person of the late most noble Grand Duke, a devoted and selfless servant of the Throne," wrote V.F. Dzhunkovsky in his memoirs. "Everyone who knew him and had the good fortune to communicate with him, could not help but mourn this Grand Duke-knight. I personally knew the Grand Duke, who was always very kind and attentive to me; he was a rare family man, he always kept himself simple, his modesty and delicacy were extraordinary He left a particularly good memory among the pupils of military educational institutions, for whom he was a real loving father. He quite often visited schools and corps, spending whole days among pupils and showing interest not only in their successes, but also in their family life, coming to the aid of any one in need."

The Manifesto of Nicholas II dated 2nd June 1915 on the death of Grand Duke Konstantin Konstantinovich says: "The late Grand Duke Konstantin Konstantinovich devoted his life to domestic science and put a lot of work and care into the highest leadership in the military education of youth, which produced such a valiant composition of officers, and heroic deeds which in a real war will forever be imprinted in the history of the Russian army."

Grand Duke Konstantin Konstantinovich would outlive three of his sons: Ioann, Konstantin and Igor, and his brother Dmitri, all of whom were murdered by the Bolsheviks in 1918 and 1919 respectively.

He was the last of the Romanovs to die before the 1917 Revolution and the last Romanov to be buried in the Grand Ducal Tomb, which is adjacent to the SS Peter and Paul Cathedral, situated in the Peter and Paul Fortress in St. Petersburg.

The solemn funeral procession of Grand Duke Konstantin Konstantinovich, took place on 21st (O.S. 8th June 1915). A vintage newsreel exists to this day, which shows the funeral procession through the streets of Petrograd. In both the newsreel and the photo on page 16 of this book, Emperor Nicholas II can be seen walking behind the horse-drawn carriage which carries the coffin bearing the remains of the much loved grand duke.

The desecration of Kostya's tomb

During the Soviet years, the interior decoration of the Grand Ducal Mausoleum was destroyed. In the 1920s, the tombs were looted. The white marble gravestone slab of Grand Duke Konstantin was broken, and its fragments were thrown into his crypt [see photo on page 23]. A new floor was laid over the graves, few people visiting the mausoleum knew that under the new floor were the remains of members of the Imperial Family. The Grand Ducal Mausoleum became a museum in the 1950s.

In 1992, work began on the restoration of the interiors of the mausoleum. Workers excavated the floor, where they found the crypt of Grand Duke Konstantin, which was covered with three limestone slabs. A large hole was found cut in the head of one slab, and sealed with cement. No one doubted that this was the result of an attempted looting of the grave in the 1920s. Due to financial difficulties, work had to be stopped, and the clearing of the crypt from debris was delayed by two years. When opening the lower slabs, it turned out that the seams connecting the ceilings of the crypt were still in good condition. They were carefully sealed with lime mortar.

When the experts removed the last slab, they found a copper casket, in the lid of which there was an irregularly shaped hole cut with metal scissors. The location of the hole completely coincided with the hole in the lower limestone slab. It is believed that when the looters discovered that there was nothing of value inside, they abandoned the idea of grave robbing altogether.

In September 1994, the casket was raised to the surface. Aside from the skull and skeleton bones founds inside the decayed coffin boards, a number of other items were discovered, including funeral accessories, a pillow under the head, a holiday prayer on silk fabric, brushes from the cover and coffin, double-headed eagles, a pectoral cross, sheets of printed text in Latin, and two palm branches. The experts confirmed that the remains had not subjected to vandalism.

After an agreement with representatives of the clergy, it was decided to rebury the remains of the Grand Duke in a new coffin with the possible preservation of accessories found in the original coffin. An urn with the ashes of the burnt boards of the old coffin and the remains of clothes were also placed in the new coffin.

The restoration of Grand Duke Konstantin Konstantinovich's tomb was carried out, and on 22nd December 1994, his remains were reburied in the presence of his descendants, and on 15th June 1997 [see photo on page 23], a new tombstone was solemnly laid.

Fragments of the origianl marble tombstone

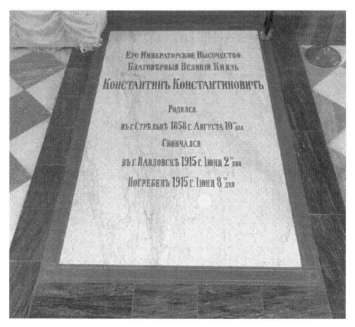

The restored tombstone of Grand Duke Konstantin Konstantinovich in the Grand Ducal Mausoleum

Formation of cadets - participants of the 19th All-Cadet Congress - at a memorial service at the grave of Grand Duke Konstantin Konstantinovich

Early 20th century postcard of the Grand Ducal Mausoleum, situated in the Peter and Paul Fortress, St. Petersburg

The rector of the church of the Valaam Monastery, Father Nikolai, performed a *panikhída* [memorial service], and the re-burial of the remains took place.

In memory of the "Father of all cadets", foreign cadet associations collected the necessary amount of money to restore the marble tombstone on the grave of the Grand Duke. On 15th June 1997, on the 82nd anniversary of his death, the slab was solemnly consecrated. A delegation of 17 foreign cadets arrived in St. Petersburg for this historic event [see photo on page 24]. One of the participants in this event, E. S. Yusupov, wrote: "At the head of the slab is a portrait of the Grand Duke, flowers around, birch branches on the floor. The guard of honour stood with historical military banners. Nearby are Suvorov, Nakhimov, and Cadets with candles in their hands. Do they understand what's going on here? The memorial service has attracted such a large number of people, the first such event to take place in 82 years, according to church clergy.

To this day, few people know that at the turn of the bloodiest century for Russia, the peace of the august poet was disturbed. But let's hope that no one will ever disturb the eternal sleep of one of the most worthy representatives of the Russian Imperial Family."

PAUL GILBERT
30 March 2022

AWARDS and MEDALS

Grand Duke Konstantin Konstantinovich received the following Russian decorations:

Russian

Order of St. Andrew, 1st Class, 1858
Order of St. Alexander Nevsky, 1858
Order of St. Anna, 1st Class, 1858
Order of the White Eagle, 1865
Order of St. Stanislaus, 1st Class, 1865
Order of St. George, 4th Class, 1877
Order of St. Vladimir, 4th Class, 1883; 3rd Class, 14 May 1896; 2nd Class, 1903; 1st Class, 1913

NOTES:

[1] Some contemporary historians often refer to Grand Duke Konstantin Konstantinovich as Nicholas II's uncle, however, this is incorrect, they are first cousins.
[2] Advocacy of Slavic and specifically Russian culture over western European culture especially as practiced among some members of the Russian intelligentsia in the middle 19th century
[3] During her visit to Russia in 1884, the future Grand Duchess Elizaveta Mavrikievna, announced that she wished to keep her Lutheran faith, which was a serious blow for her future husband, since Konstantin believed firmly in the

Russian Orthodox Church. Even worse was the fact that she refused to kiss the cross held in Orthodox services. The couple's children were all raised in the Orthodox faith.

[4] Following his death in 1915, the diaries of the Grand Duke, were transferred to the archive of the Russian Academy of Sciences with the condition of publication no earlier than 90 years after his death (published in Russian 1994). His diaries have not been published in English.

[5] Prince Bagration-Muhransky (1889-1915) married Grand Duke Konstantin's eldest daughter Princess of the Imperial blood Tatiana Konstantinovna. The couple were married at Pavlovsk on 24 August 1911, in the presence of Emperor Nicholas II. Their happiness, however, was short-lived, the prince died in battle on 20 May 1915, he was only 26 years old.

[6] Grand Duke Konstantin's eldest sister Grand Duchess Olga Konstantinovna (1851-1926), who was queen consort of Greece as the wife of King George I. She was briefly the regent of Greece in 1920.

The only monument to Grand Duke Konstantin Konstantino-vich was established at the Military Academy in Odessa in 1999. It was dismantled on 27 November 2015, as part of a "decommunization process" established in Ukraine, which "outlawed communist and Soviet symbols, in addition to those of the Russian Empire as well.

Grand Duke Konstantin Konstantinovich

Grand Duke Konstantin
Konstantinovich at Pavlovsk

by Alexei N. Guzanov
Translated by Julia Denne

The 140th anniversary of the birth of Grand Duke Konstantin Konstantinovich in 1998 was widely celebrated throughout Russia. A number of exhibitions were arranged in St. Petersburg. The Pushkin House (the Institute of Russian Language and Literature of the Academy of Sciences and Humanities) hosted a research conference. The exhibition in the Pavlovsk Palace, now a museum called "Grand Duke Konstantin Konstantinovich, the owner of Pavlovsk" mounted in partnership with the State Archive of the Russian Federation, and the exhibitions in the National Library of Russia and in the Strelna Palace, were the most interesting exhibitions. The opening of part of the residential premises of Grand Duke Konstantin Konstantinovich in the Marble Palace was a significant event of spring 1998. The Congress of the Russian Association of Former Military Cadets, held in St. Petersburg and devoted to the memory of Grand Duke Konstantin Konstantinovich, was another important event.

Konstantin Konstantinovich was an outstanding personality. His talent, creative work, state and public activities served the benefit of his country. In 1889 he was appointed President of the Imperial Academy of Sciences and Humanities. In that capacity he made every effort to do his best. He initiated a number of progressive reforms and did a lot for the development of Russian academic research. In 1889 he headed a commission on the celebration of the centenary of the famous Russian poet Alexander Pushkin. He headed and participated in the work of many research commissions, served as President of the Russian Archeology Society, as well as the Temperance Society. He was an active member and an honorary member of a number of organisations, including the Imperial Russian Music Society, the Imperial Society for the Encouragement of the Arts, the Moscow Society of Nature Researchers, the Imperial Society of Devotees of Natural Sciences, Anthropology and Ethnography, the Life Guards Society, the Society of Devotees of the Russian Language, and the Orthodox Palestinian Society.

Pavlovsk was a favourite place of Grand Duke Konstantin Konstantinovich, and it was the place where he died in 1915. An excerpt from the memoirs by Baron N. V. Drizen confirms that "... the Grand Duke adored his Pavlovsk. He knew the history of every bush, every path and enjoyed talking about them. Maybe that is why Pavlovsk, more than any other suburb of St. Petersburg, retained the character of an 'intelligent relic of the old days'. Taking care of his estate made the Grand Duke go to extremes. The Pavlovsk Palace is still being illuminated with oil lamps. They do not have electricity over there." (*Baron N. V. Drizen. Meeting K.R. History Bulletin, December 1916.*) Grand Duke Konstantin Konstantinovich used to write about his love and adoration for this really unusual and magnificent place in his diary: "After 1 p.m. Mother and I rode horses to Pavlovsk! How happy I was to see dear Pavlovsk, which I like so much, which combines so many fine memories. Every path, building, tree are so dear, familiar and remind of the best. We came to the palace. The bell started ringing, and yellow lancer guards came running. Mitya and I ran to our rooms. Even the smell is the same, I remember this smell by heart ... I think how much I will enjoy showing Pavlovsk to Elisabeth if she will be my wife." (Pavlovsk, August 14, 1882.)

The Pavlovsk palace and park ensemble is an outstanding monument to Russian decorative arts and occupies an important place in the history of Russia. In 1777 Empress Catherine II gave a hunting estate adjoining her summer residence in Tsarskoe Selo to her son Grand Duke Paul Petrovich and his wife Maria Fedorovna as a gift to celebrate the birth of their first son Alexander (the future Emperor Alexander I). In 1782 the construction of the Large Stone Palace, designed by the Scottish architect Charles Cameron, started. Such famous architects as V. Brenna, A. Voronikhin, J. Quarenghi and K. Rossi took part in the construction and decoration of the palace. The same year, 1782, the Grand Duke and his wife went to Europe, and their trip lasted for almost thirteen months. On this trip they acquired a great number of fine pieces of decorative art and crafts, as well as paintings and antiques. As a result of this trip and the following elaborate designs of the palace interior and its collections, Pavlovsk becme a unique well-balanced artistic ensemble.

After the death of Emperor Paul I in 1801, Pavlovsk became a favourite summer residence of his widow Empress Maria Fedorovna. She did her best to retain the primordial image of Pavlovsk. After her death in 1828, she bequeathed Pavlovsk to her third son Michael Pavlovich, who owned it until he died in 1849. As he did not have any heirs, the second son of Emperor Nicholas I, Grand Duke Konstantin, became the owner of Pavlovsk. Konstantin Nikolaevich liked Pavlovsk. He introduced several changes. He was an important state figure and a politician. He headed the State Council, the Navy Ministry, as well as other state and public organisations. In 1861-1863, he was Vice-regent of Poland. Konstantin Nikolaevich was married to a German princess Alexandra Frederica of Saxe-Altenburg (Alexandra Iosifovna, after she was converted to the Orthodox religion).

They had six children – four sons and two daughters.

Grand Duke Konstantin Konstantinovich was their second son. He was born in 1858 in the Strelna Palace and was a gifted child from birth. He received the best education at home. Being a son of the General Admiral of the Russian fleet, at 12 he was a naval cadet and made a voyage around the world on board the frigate *Svetlana*, which was part of the squadron under the command of Grand Duke Alexis Alexandrovich. In 1876 the squadron visited New York. His father predestined a naval career for his son. Konstantin Konstantinovich took part in the Russo-Turkish War of 1877-1878 as a warrant officer where he received St. George Cross, his first order, for destroying a Turkish ship. But then, being of poor health, he had to leave the navy. He continued to serve his country in the Lifeguards Division of the Izmailovsky regiment. In 1884 he organised there a literary society called *Ismailovsky Leisure*. It was a very unusual event in the army. Konstantin Konstantinovich was not only its founder, but he was its president and an active member. At the meetings literary and musical works were performed. Konstantin Konstantinovich frequently read his own work and took part in the theatrical performances. In 1907 the 25th anniversary of the literary activity of Grand Duke Konstantin Konstantinovich was celebrated by the *Ismailovsky Leisure* society. In honour of this anniversary Konstantin Konstanti-novich received a record book made by Faberge. It was a leather book, 18X13 cm, with silver plates. There was a golden lyre on a white enamel background in the upper medallion, and an in-scription around it on a red background, saying "Ismailovsky Leisure. 1884". In the central me-dallion there was a monogram "K. R.", and num-bers XXV in the lower medallion. The silver plates were decorated with eight rubies. On the flyleaf of the book was a white enamel medallion with the inscription: "In the name of courage, kindness and beauty", Monogram "K.R." and dates 1882-1907. On the silver plates one can see the stamp of A. Richter. The album contains 40 pages of manuscript poems by Grand Duke Konstantin Konstantinovich. The book is now part of the col-lection of the Pavlovsk museum. Konstantin Kon-stantinovich wrote in his diary about this present: "...at the end Porezky, on behalf of the regiment, gave me a leather record book with Faberge silver plates, a Leisure token inserted into the leather, and red enameled letters of my pen name K.R. on the back."

Grand Duke Konstantin Konstantinovich's diaries are kept at the State Archive of the Rus-sian Federation in Moscow. There are 1,393 files in his personal archive containing, besides dia-ries, many other documents related to his career and literary work. From 1884 until 1891 Kon-stantin Konstantinovich was the company commander of the Guards of the Izmailovsky regiment. From 1891 until 1900 he was the commander of Lifeguards of the Preobrazhensky regiment. After that he was appointed Chief Commander of military educational institutions, then he was made a Lieutenant General, and later on he was an Inspector General of military educational institutions. However, while serving his country in the army as best as he could, he was in his heart always interested in poetry, literature and music.

Konstantin Konstantinovich started to write poetry when he was twenty years old. Being a member of the Emperor's family, he could not put his full name under his poems. That is why he had to use the pen name K. R. (Konstantin Romanov). "These two dear letters are like two bright fires in the autumn darkness, they call for me to go forward without roads", wrote a famous Russian poet A. Maikov about K.R. In his childhood Konstantin Konstantinovich often went to Pavlovsk and liked it a lot. The magnificent Pavlovsk park with its poetical spots, Russian nature, romantic park pavilions, the palace with its history, splendid interior decorations and collections could not but have a great influence on the child's exalted soul. In Pavlovsk, poetry penetrates everything. Famous Russian poets and writers, such as V. Zhukovsky, Neledinsky-Melezhky, I. Krylov, F. Dostoevsky, wrote about the beauty and charm of the Pavlovsk park. Maria Fedorovna, the first owner of Pavlovsk, created the atmosphere of the beautiful, sublime and inspiring world around it. Pavlovsk, full of harmony and integrity, fascinated, attracted and energised. "One wants to start a creative life here, to get up early, to sleep less, not to waste time", wrote Konstantin Konstantinovich in his diary in August 1896.

One can understand his attitude to Pavlovsk reading the following lines from his diary: "LaRauche, a professor of music theory from the St. Petersburg conservatoire, came to see me. He is a friend of mine, and I was happy to show him around our palace; I am never bored or tired of telling the same things over and over again about various rooms, china, bronzes, trellises, antique furniture, of showing off all these splendid things to my guests..." (June 23, 1879) This is how the Grand Duke redecorated his room in Pavlovsk the same summer: "...In the morning I went upstairs to the storage rooms and looked at a pile of old things; I found Jacob armchairs and a splendid bureau. Among other junk, I found the portraits of Peter the Great and Charles I, King of England. All of it I took to my room. My mother helps me to decorate it, it looks very nice." (Pavlovsk, July 19, 1879) He always wrote about Pavlovsk, its image being somewhat of a phantom. Another abstract from the diary: "... Came home from the backyard; I admired the look of the palace in this clear light June night with a full moon." (June 23, 1879) Or "I went with Tatiana Michaelovna through the rooms of the palace having a list with the description of rooms made by Maria Fedorovna, and we admired the wonderful things." (Pavlovsk, July 17, 1879)

After his father, Grand Duke Konstantin Nikolaevich, died in 1892, Konstantin Konstantinovich inherited Pavlovsk, as his elder brother Nicholas Constantinovich was declared mentally ill, sent to Tashkent where he died in 1918, and deprived of his inheritance rights. The reason for his exile was the scandalous fact that he stole the framework decorated with precious stone from his mother's icon and sold it to buy jewelry for his lover, an American adventuress, named Fanny Lear. But the worst part of it was his perjury when an innocent person was blamed for the theft. Thus, Konstantin Konstantinovich became the owner of the Pavlovsk, Strelna and Marble palaces. Let us look again into his diary: "Though after the death of my father I own Pavlovsk (Nicholas, being incompetent, lost its rights), up to now I haven't felt myself its owner...I participated only a little in its management...All reports are signed by my mother as well, who, though she is not the owner, was not deprived by me of her rights that she executed when my father was ill... Now I would like to look deep into the management. Yesterday for the first time I inspected local schools... What I saw made a good impression on me." (Pavlovsk, October 8, 1896)

Being the owner of Pavlovsk, Konstantin

Konstantinovich paid a lot of attention to the palace, the park, as well as the town and its charity institutions. Of course, his priority was the Pavlovsk palace. In 1896 he wrote in his diary: "Architect Zaitsev came. I went with him through the rooms of the lower floor and showed wonderfully made and beautiful things. I think about publishing drawings of Pavlovsk and its places of interest." It should be mentioned that Konstantin Konstantinovich published four issues of *Pavlovsk. The Palace. The Park.* containing copies of the best known and artistically interesting objects of art. He was interested in the Pavlovsk palace not just because it was a beautiful place. He was also interested in the history of the palace, the history of his family in the 18th century, as well as the life of his great grandmother Empress Maria Fedorovna. This remarkable woman outlived the reign of her mother-in-law Catherine II, her husband Paul I, her eldest son Alexander I and saw her other son Nicholas crowned Tsar two years before her death in 1828. The personality of Empress Maria Fedorovna made a great impression on Konstantin Konstantinovich. She showed an example of selfless work for the benefit of Russia, as she was heavily involved in charitable work. She also had very good taste in art. Konstantin Konstantinovich did his best to return Pavlovsk to the condition and appearance it had at the time of Maria Fedorovna. He wrote in his diary: "We had breakfast in rotunda (Italian room – A. G.). Then I went to the main rooms with Gering. As per my instructions, we put there all objects according to the 1849 list, when it belonged to Michael Pavlovich and everything was kept as at the time of Maria Fedorovna. All objects, described by her in 1795, are at their places." (Pavlovsk, September 9, 1907)

He really intended to return Pavlovsk to its original look, because, as time went by, a number of objects from palace collections had been placed in other rooms. Having great respect to the historic decoration of the palace, he tried not only to return the objects where they belonged, but he also tried to return and stress their meaning. For example: " After the liturgy we had breakfast in the study of Pavel I. I suggested, with the consent from my mother, to put a glass cover, used at the time of Pavel to cover the Emperor's crown when he lived in Pavlovsk, on the carved wooden stand a la Louis XVI; there are the same stands with covers in Peterhof and Gatchina. There was an ugly wooden basket full of flowers on our stand before, and I suggested to replace it with old red velvet cushions used to put the crown on, and the glass cover." (Pavlovsk, July 15, 1897) He felt very distressed when, due to various reasons, he could not do anything for Pavlovsk. "I would like to and cannot start to put the picture gallery in the Pavlovsk palace in order. The pictures are hung in an irrational order, according to their sizes rather than to the art schools. (January 30,

1911) The records in his diary dated December 27, 1910 exemplify not only his love for art, but also his responsibility as the owner of a collection of fine art, which in his opinion belonged to the country and the people, and he thought himself to be only its custodian: " I wrote a letter to the Italian Ambassador Melegari. He had written me about an exhibition of the portraits by Italian artists of the 15th – 18th centuries, to be held next year in Florence, and asked me to show there the works by Lampi that are in Pavlovsk. I had to reject his proposal, as I do not consider myself to be the owner of Pavlovsk collections: I only have an entailed estate." In his letter to Emperor Nicholas II, Grand Duke George Michaelovich also mentions the attitude of Grand Duke Konstantin Konstantinovich towards preservation and consideration for the national property: "...Yesterday I met Vladimir (Grand Duke Vladimir Alexandrovich) in the Mariinsky theatre, and I started talking about this (he means the exhibition of Russian paintings in Munich where several paintings from the museum of Emperor Alexander III were supposed to be sent, and Grand Duke Vladimir Alexandrovich supported this idea) and in a calm way advanced the reasons, and first he seemed to understand me, but later started yelling at me and got almost rude to me. Fortunately, Konstantin was also there, and he strongly supported me and quoted Pavlovsk as an example: the paintings from there are not permitted to be sent abroad. In other countries none of the first-rate museums sends pictures anywhere, and people have to come there to look at them."

Konstantin Konstantinovich also did his best to return the park to the way it looked originally, and he wrote in his diary, as follows: "...I was on the Liven island where the summerhouse was restored, and now the paths are laid again, rotting trees are felled, and new trees are planted. I would like to return the original look to this picturesque island." (Pavlovsk, September 27, 1898)

In 1884 the wedding of Grand Duke Konstantin Konstantinovich and Princess Elizabeth of Saxe-Altenburg (Elizabeth Mavrikievna) was held in Petersburg. Elizabeth Mavrikievna was not converted to the Orthodox church, but all their children were baptised and brought up according to the Orthodox traditions. In 1909 the 25th anniversary of the wedding of Konstantin Konstantinovich and Elizabeth Mavrikievna was celebrated in Pavlovsk. The celebration went on for several days. Konstantin Konstantinovich described it in his diary on April 15, as follows: " Gavrilushka and Tatiana were in charge of the garland, made with fresh flowers 14 archins long (391.3 inches) and hung on the curtain in our bedroom. The gardener converted my wife's and my studies into flowerbeds. The children let in 8 bullfinches through the nets on the windows in my study." (Pavlovsk, April 15, 1909) At noon, representatives from the town of Pavlovsk congratulated Konstantin Konstantinovich and Elizabeth Mavrikievna. Representatives from different organisations occupied different rooms.

Thus, the representatives of orphanages and schools were in the picture gallery, those of the clergy were in the gallery study, and the majority—low-rank officials, policemen, firemen, guards, etc—were in the main throne room. On behalf of the people of Pavlovsk, Gering, Chief Councilor of the Pavlovsk Township, presented them with bread and salt. There was a grand dinner later on attended by Emperor Nicholas II and his wife. On April 16, the very day of the wedding, there was a solemn liturgy. Afterwards, everyone went to Petersburg for a reception in the Marble Palace. Then, they returned to Pavlovsk. On April 17, the celebration went on in Pavlovsk.

All children took efforts to prepare for the celebration. Dressed in historical costumes, they presented in the main throne room a live picture *The Family of Emperor Paul* based on the painting by Kugelhen from the Pavlovsk collection. The painting depicted Emperor Paul, his wife Maria Fedorovna, and all their children. Konstantin Konstantinovich wrote rapturously in his diary: "The celebration turned out to be wonderful and unusual. The preparation demanded a lot of love and fine attention, and it was done secretly from us, the hosts and parents." (Pavlovsk, April 17, 1909) The children also presented a performance *The Wedding of the Sun and Spring.* Fifty-two children, including all the children of the happy couple, took part in the performance. The following is what Oleg Constantinovich wrote in his diary: " The emperor was expected to enter any minute. The stage was quiet...We heard the approaching steps of the tsar's family, and *Glory* started. Everybody was delighted to listen to this Russian song, to feel devotion to the Emperor who was so close by, but being nervous before the performance was enough to give us the shivers... Here is the Emperor sitting dressed in his infantry uniform, the Empress, and a little tsarevich on her knees... In general the performance went well, and the audience was pleased... After the end of the performance, mother, father and the guests gathered in the picture gallery to wait for the procession of flowers, bugs, birds and other performers. All of them walked by mother and father with flowers in their hands and put flowers by their feet." There were two platinum rings among numerous gifts. The Romanov family presented silver plates with the name of the person who gave the gift engraved on the back of each plate.

Thanks to Konstantin Konstantinovich, the artistic life in Pavlovsk was eventful. As his children grew older, they started to take part in various activities and to develop a number of new ideas and initiatives. "We are glad and amused by the excitement, which came into the Pavlovsk palace with the growing children, as well as with other unplanned occasions: literary and musical evenings, my military anniversaries... It is fun to make lists of guests, to hustle about making the best possible arrangements for the evening, dinner or reception, to send invitations, to prepare carriages for it, to arrange buffet meals, to decorate rooms. The children, our ladies and all our people participate in making lists of guests. My wife and I always greet the guests – she stands on the upper landing and I am on the upper stairs, the children take turns in taking them into the rooms where the party is. The performances are held in the ballroom: the stage is large, and though it takes a lot of space there is enough room for an audience of 150 people." (January 11, 1909) "The Emperor may have liked it here, he did not miss any evenings...My performance took place on the 16th and was a great success. The Emperor and the audience were very pleased, especially with the performance of Henry IV... Later on, the Emperor repeated several times that I made great success during the last 10 years and that Henry IV made a great impression on him." (March 14-18, 1910)

Konstantin Konstantinovich and Elizabeth Mavrikievna had nine children. The first son Ioann was born in 1886. It should be mentioned that the children of Grand Duke Konstantin Konstantinovich did not have titles of Grand Dukes, but, as per the reforms made by Emperor Alexander III, they each had a title of "Duke or Prince of the Emperor's Family", inasmuch as only the children and grandchildren of the reigning Emperor could have the title of Grand Duke. Alexander III had to carry out these reforms due to the fact that by the end of the 19th century the Emperor's family had expanded considerably. As the result of the reform, the Dukes of the Emperor's Family were entitled to receive only a single-payment grant from the treasury in the amount of one million rubles, while the Grand Dukes received annual payments in the amount of 280,000 rubles. Ioann, Konstantin Konstantinovich's first son, was very religious. He served in the Lifeguards Division of the Horsemen regiment, where he was humourously called "Ioann the Funeral Service", because he was sent more often than anybody else to participate in the official funeral services for members of the families of European monarchs.

In 1911 Ioann married Elena, the daughter of Peter, the king of Serbia. She was two years his senior. In 1914 their son Vsevolod was born and in 1915 their daughter Catherine. Ioann Constantinovich died in July 1918, together with other members of the Romanov family, when he was thrown alive into a mine. Later he was canonised by the Orthodox church.

In 1887 Gavril, the second son of Konstantin Konstantinovich, was born. Gavril Constantinovich with the support of Maxim Gorky managed to leave Russia in 1918. He died in 1955 and was buried on the Russian cemetry Saint Jenevieve de

Bois. His published book of memoirs *In the Marble Palace* was published in Russian, French and English editions.

In 1890 their first daughter Tatiana was born. She married the Georgian Duke Konstantin Bagration-Mukhransky, who died in 1915 during the First World War near Lviv. Tatiana Constantinovna left Russia in the autumn of 1918 together with her two children Teymuraz and Natalia. In 1920 she married Alexander Vasilievich Karachentsev, who was a manager for Grand Duke Dmitry Constantinovich. But their marriage was a short one, as Karachentsev died from diphteria in 1921. Tatiana Constantinovna lived in Switzerland until 1946, when she became a nun and took the name Tamara. She became prioress of the Russian Eleosky Convent in Jerusalem. She died in 1970.

In 1890 their third son Konstantin was born. He died in July 1918, together with other members of the Romanov family, when he was thrown alive into a mine by the Communists. He was canonised by the Orthodox church.

Then in 1892 his son Oleg was born. After he graduated from the Alexandrovsky Lyceum, he served in the Lifeguards Division of the Hussar regiment. He died from a mortal wound he got during military operation near Vilna. He was buried, according to his will, in his father's Moscow estate Ostashevo. He was awarded the St. George Cross for bravery. Oleg Constantinovich, more than the other children, was spiritually close to his father. He was also very interested in literature and poetry. He wrote poems and short stories.

Igor was born in 1894. He died in July 1918, together with other members of the Romanov family, when he was thrown alive into a mine by the Communists. He was canonised by the Orthodox church.

George was born in 1903. He died in 1937 in New York.

Natalia lived only for a few months after she was born in 1905.

Princess Vera was born in 1906. She died in the United States in January 2001.

Grand Duchess Elizabeth Mavrikievna left Russia in November 1918 for Stockholm, where she found refuge provided by the Swedish King and Queen for herself, her two children, George and Vera, and her two grandchildren, Vsevolod and Catherine. Later she moved to Brussels, and then to her native town Altenburg in Germany where she died in 1927 and was buried in her family burial vault.

Konstantin Konstantinovich and his family liked to spend time in Pavlovsk not only during summer, but also sometimes in winter. "We intend to spend winter in Pavlovsk again, so it makes sense to have our best piano forte here." (Pavlovsk, September 10, 1907)

The Emperor Nicholas II and his family used

to visit Konstantin Konstantinovich from time to time. Gavril Constantinovich described in his memoirs one of the balls in the Pavlovsk Palace, as follows: "The Emperor and the Empress arrived in the middle of the ball. Father greeted the Empress with a bouquet of flowers. The ball was in the Large Dancing Room... There was a special corner there, decorated with antique furniture and plants, for the Empress. Mother introduced female guests to the Empress. But the Empress did not stay for long... Our parents danced quadrille. Father looked very graceful in the cavalry uniform...

When it grew dark, lamps and candles were lit in the rooms. In the dancing room there were candles around the curtain rods. When they were lit, they made a spectacular view. Four glass lights with lit candles came from the ceiling. There was no electricity in Pavlovsk at that time. It was installed on my initiative in 1911 or 1912 in the bedrooms, but it was never installed in the main rooms.

After the ball, we had dinner in the Greek Room and nearby rooms."

Grand Duke Konstantin Konstantinovich also paid a lot of attention to the town of Pavlovsk. The town was small, but it had its own Chief Councilor of the Township. There were several different churches in the town. The Pavlovsk musical railroad station attracted a lot people. As the town was part of the entailed estate, all town affairs were confirmed and agreed upon by the Grand Duke. In the beginning of the 20th century the railroad, which used to end in Pavlovsk, was extended further on till Vitebsk, and a new station Pavlovsk II was built. In 1910 the skating ring building was erected, which in 1911 was reconstructed to house a cinema theatre called 'Moulin Rouge'. In 1911 Grand Duke Konstantin Konstantinovich gave a land parcel for the first electric power station in Pavlovsk, and the same year there were electric lights in the town. The Konstantin Magnet and Meteorology Observatory of the Academy of Sciences and Humanities, founded by Grand Duke Konstantin Nikolaevich, continued to operate in Pavlovsk. In 1897, in the small community within the boundaries of Pavlovsk, called Tsarskaya Slavyanka, Olginsky Orphanage was opened, named after Olga, daughter of Emperor Nicholas II, who was born in 1896. The Emperor, who was present at the opening ceremony together with the Empress, sponsored the orphanage. In 1909 Captain O. Pentyukhin organised the first team of boy scouts called *Beaver.*

Afterwards, this movement expanded all over the country. In 1902, the new St. Nicholas Cathedral, built to replace an old dilapidated wooden church, was consecrated. The cathedral was designed by the architect von Gauguin in the traditional Russian style. Brick, specially ordered from France, covered the exterior walls. The crosses on the cathedral were also quite unusual. They were gilded with inserted facetted crystal plates, which sparkled in the sunlight. The cathedral interior was beautifully decorated as well. The iconostasis was made of light oaks, and the icons were painted on china. But the pride of the cathedral was its magnificent bells cast in the St. Petersburg's Orlov factory. The largest bell weighed 169 poods (2,768 kg). It should be mentioned that Konstantin Konstantinovich rejected two designs of the cathedral, and it was his suggestion to commission the architect von Gauguin, whose design was finally approved. In 1913, in the honour of the 300-year anniversary of the Romanovs, two more churches were founded: the St. Trinity Church and the Transfiguration Church. Grand Duke Konstantin Konstantinovich gave the land parcel for the former church. The architect A. Ilyin designed it. It was suggested that this church could become a burial vault for the owners of Pavlovsk. The latter was founded in the village of Tyarlevo, near the park, designed by the architect A. Zakharov. Unfortunately, both churches suffered a lot during the Soviet period and were partially rebuilt. One of them houses the fire station, the other – a weaving mill.

Emperor Nicholas II frequently mentions his visits to Pavlovsk in his diary. He used to walk in the Pavlovsk Park, or ride there in a carriage, and sometimes rode a horse. He wrote in his diary on May 17, 1895: " At 7:30 we went to Pavlovsk to have dinner with Costya and Mavra. We took a look at the upper level of this beautiful and interesting palace. We stayed in the lower rooms until 10:30." On October 24, 1896 he wrote: "I walked alone and at 4:25 went with Alex to Pavlovsk, where we had tea with Costya and Mavra. Returned home on a cold night full of stars at 6:30." When Nicholas II acquired automobiles, he frequently went to Pavlovsk by automobile. As he says in his diary: "...we motored to Pavlovsk."

The study of Grand Duke Konstantin Konstantinovich in Pavlovsk was on the ground floor of the palace in the former White Dining Room, designed by the Scottish architect Cameron. It is the largest room on the ground floor. Three glass doors overlook the west porch, which has a view of the park towards the Slavyanka river. As designed by Cameron, the pilasters of the Corinthian order and a molding frieze decorated the room. In 1858 this room was redecorated for use as the reception room for Grand Duchess Alexandra Iosifovna. At that time large mirrors were inserted into all three doors, covering the whole surface, which gave it the name of "the Mirror Room". On July 4, 1896 Konstantin Konstantinovich wrote in his diary: "At 1 O'clock I went to Pavlovsk. We had breakfast with Mother, my wife, Vera and her daughters on the balcony. The weather is heavenly. I decided to move my study to the Large Mirror Room, and I spent time sorting things out over there. This room is much lighter, more comfortable and beautiful." Two years later he wrote in the letter to Grand Duke Sergei Alexandrovich: "We lead a quiet and pleasant life here, and thanks be to God, are not going anywhere. My huge room – a lower room converted into the study – becomes more beautiful and comfortable. Antique Pavlovsk furniture, covered with cloths from Sapozhnikov, is placed very conveniently; in the evenings of the dark cold autumn time, the cheerful fire brightly sparkles in the large rooms."

"In the evening I worked in my dear huge study. This is the largest, the most beautiful and my favourite room among all three palaces: Pavlovsk, Marble and Strelnya." (K. R. diary, August 11, 1900, the State Archive of the Russian Federation) Konstantin Konstantinovich did not make any changes in this room, only redecorated it. He even moved there a bronze statue of a Borgese warrior from the park. (Now the statue is on its original place in the park, where it was at the time of Maria Fedorovna.) He also moved there the furniture he liked from the other rooms in the palace. Following the fashion and artistic tastes of that time, the study was overcrowded with different things, photographs and souvenirs. Almost none of his personal belongings survived, except for some separate pieces, such as: an armchair with arms that look like swans, made in the beginning of the 20th century; the sofa on which he died, his record book described before, silver stamps with red stone handles, and a china set manufactured at the Imperial China Factory, with views of Pavlovsk and consisting of eight pieces – a large tray, two cups with saucers, a tea pot, a sugar basin, and a creamer. The china paintings were done by Yakov Goriaev, based on the drawings by V. Zhukovsky. The set was made in 1914 – 1915.

Konstantin Konstantinovich died in his favourite Pavlovsk palace on June 2, 1915. His son Gavril in his book *In the Marble Palace* quoted the letter written by his sister Vera in 1941, in which she described her father's death. "I remember that in the evening aunt Olga read in Russian to Papa and me, to introduce me to the Russian literature. Papa was in bed after the latest attack of angina pectoris. On June 15 Papa and I waited for aunt Olga for a long time, as she was delayed in her infirmary because of the surgery of the wounded. I was sitting on the sofa near the pianoforte, in front of the enclosure, in father's big comfortable study in Pavlovsk. I remember quite well that I was reading a Russian translation of Goethe's "Reinecke Fuchs" by Hitrolis when I heard Papa start choking. When I heard these terrible noises three or four times, I rushed to mother's bedroom, where she tried on a new bright dress, probably, for Ostashevo, where we were going to go, since Papa was getting much better after a very strong attack of angina pectoris. In such moments of fear, a person gets much stronger. Mama could never understand how I was able to open the heavy door with a mirror and green plants in front of it, the door between mother's and father's studies. Coming to mother, I screamed, being out of breath, "Papa hat keine luft!" Mother ran with me, but it was too late. She called Arakcheev (an old valet of father's) who did not move and stood with a silly smile on his face, probably, stiffened with horror."

Emperor Nicholas II wrote in his diary about those mournful days: "June 2, Tuesday. I received Sazonov. After his report, little George Constantinovich came in and told me about Costya's death. At 9:25 I went to Pavlovsk for the first funeral service. Aunt Olga, Mavra and Mitya attended the service. None of the adult sons." On June 3, Wednesday: "After lunch we went to Pavlovsk for the funeral service." On June 4, Thursday: "Went to Pavlovsk. The funeral service was upstairs, in the round room." On June 5, Friday: "After lunch we went to Pavlovsk for the funeral service. All family was there." On June 6, Saturday: "At 2 o'clock I arrived in Pavlovsk for the funeral service, together with Olga, Tatiana and Mary. Afterwards, the coffin was carried downstairs and put on the gun carriage. I went with the procession round the corner and returned to Tsarskoe Selo. Went for a walk. At 4 o'clock we went to the city. Mother and the rest of the family waited for the arrival of the funeral train, which came in ten minutes. The procession moved past the cathedral of the Semenovsky regiment, along Gorokhovaya street and Fontanka embankment, through Mars Field and the Trinity bridge. We came to the fortress at 7:10, and after the funeral service returned to Tsarskoe Selo at 8:30. Very tired." On June 8, Monday: "At 10:10 went to the city, directly to the Peter and Paul Cathedral, with Ella, Olga, Tatiana and Maria. The funeral service and singing went on for two and half-hours. It was sad to look at aunt Olga, Mavra, and especially poor Tatiana Constantinovna, when Costya's body was put into the grave!"

In the Pavlovsk palace, on the first floor, where the main rooms are located, there is a small room between the Upper Hall and the Emperor Paul Dressing Room—the Valet Room. Above the Valet Room, there is a small attic. That is where the body of Grand Duke Konstantin Konstantinovich was embalmed. The last funeral services in the Pavlovsk Palace took place in the Italian Room, which was decorated in a mournful style. At the head of the coffin there were three flags: Admiral, Vice Admiral and Rear Admiral. The coffin was covered with gilded brocaded throw edged with ermine. Church chandeliers with lit candles surrounded the coffin. Konstantin Konstantinovich was buried in the Peter and Paul Cathedral in St. Petersburg, in the Grand Dukes' burial vault.

Nowadays, there are two portraits in the collection of Pavlovsk museum – the portrait of

Grand Duke Konstantin Konstantinovich and his wife Grand Duchess Elizabeth Mavrikievna, painted on canvas by O. Braz in 1912. The portraits were made on the request of their son, Oleg Constantinovich, and given to him on his coming of age, on November 15, 1912. Oleg Constantinovich put the portraits in his study in the Marble Palace. Grand Duke Konstantin Konstantinovich and Grand Duchess Elizabeth Mavrikievna are portrayed in the interior of the Pavlovsk Palace. Elizabeth Mavrikievna was depicted sitting in the armchair in front of the desk of Emperor Paul I in the Carpet Study. Oleg Constantinovich wrote in the letter to his father: "I jumped from the bed and, wearing only a shirt, stood for a long time and looked at your portraits. I like your portrait more: it is amazingly life-like. Many people say that only the head is too large in proportion to the body. The rest say that everything is good, except for the background. In the background you can see some door with golden stripes. Mother's portrait has not dried yet, so it is difficult to evaluate it. First I thought that she does not look life-like, but now it seems more and more that there is a lot of likeness." (According to the book *Prince Oleg* by Kulman, St. Petersburg, 1915)

Grand Duke Konstantin Konstantinovich
and Emperor Nicholas II

Grand Duke Konstantin Nikolayevich (1827–1892)
Father of Grand Duke Konstantin Konstantinovich

Grand Duchess Alexandra Iosifovna (1830-1911),
born Princess Alexandra of Saxe-Altenburg

A meeting of brothers. Grand Dukes Nikolai (left) and Konstantin Konstantinovich (right), during the latter's visit to Turkestan in 1911. In the center is Nikolai's wife - Nadezhda Alexandrovna Dreyer.

Grand Duke Konstantin Konstantinovich
and his wife Grand Duchess Elizaveta Mavrikievna

Grand Duchess Alexandra Iosifovna (born Princess Alexandra Friederike Henriette of Saxe-Altenburg, 1830-1911) with her son Grand Duke Konstantin Konstantinovich (1858-1915) and her daughter Grand Duchess Olga Konstantinovna (1851-1926, wife of King George I of Greece)

This is a truly wonderful family photo featuring 14 members of the Konstantinovichi branch of the Romanovs, taken in the garden of the Konstantin Palace at Strelna in 1903

Seated on the left is Grand Duke Dimitri Konstantinovich (1860-1919), his brother Grand Duke Konstantin Konstantinovich (1858-1915) standing behind his eldest daughter Princess of the Imperial Blood Tatiana (1890–1979); Konstantin's wife Grand Duchess Elizabeth Mavrikievna (1865-1927) is standing second from the right.

Seated in the wheelchair is Konstantin and Dimitri's mother Grand Duchess Alexandra Iosifovna (1830-1911), her 2 daughters Grand Duchesses Olga (1851-1926) and Vera (1854-1912) Konstantinovna are seen standing behind her.

Konstantin's 6 sons: Princes of the Imperial Blood Ioann, Gabriel, Konstantin, Oleg, Igor and Georgy are also depicted.

Grand Duke Konstantin Konstantinovich and Grand Duchess Elizabeth Mavrikievna had 9 children, Princess Natalia died at exactly two months in 1905. Princess Vera is absent from this photo, as she was not born until 1906.

Grand Duke Konstantin Konstantinovich and Grand Duchess Elizabeth Mavrikievna, with their eight children. Princess Vera is sitting on her father's lap. Pavlovsk, 1909.

Grand Duke Konstantin Konstantinovich and Grand Duchess Elizabeth Mavrikievna, with their eight children.

The eight children of Grand Duke Konstantin Konstantinovich
and Grand Duchess Elizabeth Mavrikievna. 1906

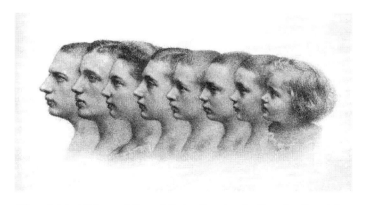

The eight children of Grand Duke Konstantin Konstantinovich
and Grand Duchess Elizabeth Mavrikievna. From left to right:
Ioann, Gabriel, Tatiana, Konstantin, Oleg, Igor, George and
Vera.

Grand Duke Konstantin Konstantinovich

- II -

The August Poet:
Grand Duke Konstantin Konstantinovich

by Zoia Beliakova

Grand Duke Konstantin Konstantinovich was born in Strelna on the 10th of August 1858, his godfather being Emperor Alexander II and his godmother the Empress Marie Alexandrovna. Of all the Romanovs, this boy was the least suited to a career in military service. A romantic, and a dreamer, he had a passion for music, poetry and the theatre. His father's house, with its musical and theatrical Fridays and marvelous rooms, where leaders, diplomats, actors, academics, and voyagers would meet for relaxed conversations, proved fertile ground for the development of the natural gifts of the young Konstantin.

As with all the Romanovs, Konstantin's upbringing and education began early. His father personally made sure that, apart from his course in the main subjects of science and languages, his tutors and professors completed a program in the history of the arts and literature. It is possible that this liberal secretly wished for Konstantin and Dmitri to study at the Moscow University, but alas, he officially stuck to the letter of the law: the Romanovs were destined for military service. The teachers of Konstantin Jr. were the famous historians Bestuzhev-Riumum and Solovyov, the pianist Küdinger, the cellist Zeifert, and the historian of music Laroche. From a young age the boy demonstrated an excellent ear for music. He would play for hours, either on the piano or on the cello. Later, he would not only play brilliantly during home concerts, but also, in summertime for the public, together with his father under the baton of the public's idol Johann Strauss in the Kursaal (Vauxhall) of Pavlovsk. The piano stood in the Gothic Room on the ground floor, and Rudolph Küdinger (Rudy) would come once a week to teach His Highness to play, and usually stayed to lunch. Konstantin Konstantinovich was particularly good at performing the Chopin preludes. He also composed music to his own poems as well as those of others. At a concert in 1889, Konstantin played Mozart in such a venerating, nearly worshiping manner that Anton Rubinstein commented, that "grand dukes are able to be artists but the latter never become grand dukes."

The master of the house was later friendly with Tchaikovsky, and he kept over three hundred letters form their correspondence. Several of the Grand Duke's most famous poems had already become popular romances in his lifetime, having been set to music by renowned composers such as Tchaikovsky, Glazunov,

Rachmaninov, Glier, and Grechaninov. In later life, as the President of the Russian Musical Society, Konstantin gave considerable assistance to young composers, making regular contributions to the upkeep of a dining room for the students of the Conservatory. Apart from Tchaikovsky, other participants appearing in the concerts at the Marble Palace included the Rubinstein brothers, Glazunov, and a host of other performers.

His interest in literature made itself apparent at an early age. In 1878 he became acquainted with Feodor Dostoevsky, and the Grand Duke read *The Idiot* and *Crime and Punishment* in raptures. Anna Grigorievna Dostoevsky wrote in her diary that "at that time [Konstantin] was a young man, sincere and good, who astonished my husband with his ardent attitude towards everything beautiful and a real love of national literature. Feodor Mikhailovich saw a genuine poetic gift in the Grand Duke." A twenty-two year old Konstantin wrote, in his diary entry on the 26th of February 1880, focusing on Dostoevsky's visit to the Marble Palace. "The evening began at 9 o'clock in the Raspberry corner study and it went off very successfully. To use Leo Tolstoi's expression, "we served Dostoevsky to his admirers like a refined dish." The Grand Duke listened attentively to the writer's low-life tale of the execution of the terrorist Mlodetsky, who had made an attempt on the life of Loris-Melikov.

Dostoevsky, under the gaze of his audience, virtually re-lived his own aborted execution of 1849, and Konstantin attempted to comprehend his feelings. A year later, the burial of Dostoevsky would be attended by the twenty-year old Grand Duke Dmitri Konstantinovich (Grand Duke Konstantin sent his condolences from Naples.) It was the first time a member of the Imperial Family had attended the funeral of a famous Russian writer.

When Ivan Turgenev arrived in Petersburg in 1880, he was besieged with invitations from the fashionable salons and from students, and was invited to the Marble Palace, where he had little success. Alexandra Iosifovna considering him to be a "red" did not leave her rooms to welcome him.

As the son of a Grand-Admiral, by family tradition, and at his father's wish, the second son was to have a career in the navy, which was to be fairly lengthy. The exam certificate of 1873 recording young Konstantin's progress in serving on the "Gilian" corvette shows nothing too impressive: three 'very good' marks in rowing, signaling and technical terminology, three 'good', the half of marks - 'fair' and *slabo'* (less than fair) in launching safety boats, rigging, and artillery skills. Due to his poor health Konstantin left the fleet, which was of great discontentment to his father. Later, Konstantin commanded the Life-Guards, in the Izmailovsky Regiment, where his friendliness and simplicity won him popularity with the Guard's officers.

This period marked Konstantin's passionate preoocupation with literature. In the Izmailovsky Regiment the "*Izmailovsky Dossughi* (Celebrations)", a literary and dramatic society, was organized, where young officers read poems and prose and performed plays. Their commander was the first to read his own verses. They met once a week, invited famous poets and writers, and were often visited by Apollon Maikov, Yakov Polonsky and Ivan Goncharov. Musicians, actors and academics took part in the "Dossughi." The actor Davydov read from the classics and helped as a stage director. The lawyer Anatol Koni told stories gathered during his legal experience.

Grand Duke Konstantin published several collections of lyrical poetry and translations under his initials K.R. He did not receive his father's blessing in his poetical enterprises, as the latter was somewhat embarrassed by a poet-son. He recounted an episode from his own life: Once, his father, Emperor Nicholas I, having found out that his son Konstantin had written a poem under the influence of Schiller's ballads, commented cuttingly: "Mon fils - mort plus tot que poete: ("Rather my son dead, than a poet"). But the wayward son and grandson became a brother-in-poetry to Apollon Maikov, Afanasii Fet, Yakov Polonsky, and Sergei Apukhtin. Many of his sonnets and elegies show the date and place in which the work was written: Pavlovsk, Ostashevo, the Marble Palace, Strelna. Apart from poems, K.R. wrote essays about modern poetry and translated works from foreign languages by Alfred de Müussey and Goethe, (*"Ifighenia in the Tauride"*). His translation of *Hamlet*, with the active participation of his wife, took twelve years (1889-1901), and was considered one of the best rendering of Shakespeare of its day. K.R. happened to get so much immersed in the text and emotions of Shakespeare's characters that he once scared his wife to death by a loud exclamation of "Queen died!". Mavra, as his wife was intimately called in the Imperial family, nearly fainted. Schiller's tragedy *"The Bride of Messina",* translated by K.R. from the German, was performed in the Chinese Theater in Tsarskoe Selo. On his thirtieth birthday K.R. wrote in his diary: "for others, I am a soldier, a company commander.... For myself, I am a poet. That is my true calling... I am not a great poet, and never will be great, as I would like to be."

Konstantin's theatrical activities are also of interest. When the participants in the "Izmailovsky Dossughi" reached a more than adequate high professional standard their productions were transferred to the Imperial Hermitage Theatre of the Winter Palace, where the female roles were played by professional actresses. The relatives of the Izmailovsky officers were invited, as well, as the elite of the capital.

Receiving a ticket was considered to be an honor. In 1888, the dress-rehearsal of *Hamlet* in K.R.'s translation, with the Grand Duke playing the Danish prince, was attended by the great tragedian Salvini for whom that part had been a climax of the repertoir. It is said that the Italian was enraptured by the acting of his most august colleague, whilst others, like Prince Sergei Volkonski, Director of the Imperial Theatres, recalled that Salvini just commented "why does he bother?... It would be so easy not to do it".

Konstantin, Jr., enjoyed masked balls and had a genuine skill and taste for making special, historically authentic costumes. The costume a la Ceaser Borgia was a great success. It was sewn for a fancy ball at the Count Sheremetev's, on Shrovetide of 1894, in accordance with Raphael's portrait at the Borgeze gallery. "Everybody praised my costume, a few people recognized Raphael's picture at once, for I deliberately hold my hands as in the picture, my right hand was on a dagger's hilt, and my left hand on my left hip", (A diary entry, February, 1894). By the way, the once Ceaser Borgia's costume was later re-modeled in a Hamlet's attire.

K.R.'s drama, *"The King of Judea"*, was staged in February of 1914. The role of Joseph of Arimithea, a member of the sanhedrin during the era of Pontius Pilate, was played by the Grand Duke. It was to be K.R.'s last appearance on the stage. The drama, written in marvelous verse and peculiar in the events interpretation, drew criticism of the Holy Synod: in *"The King of Judea"* there was no Christ, no Holy Mother, only the wives-myrrhbearers. The performances had to be called just "rehearsals," and the younger sons, princes Konstantin (as a cohort prefect) and Igor (as Ruphe) took part, as well as the choir of the elder son Ioann.

K.R.'s second son, Prince Gavriil, remembered the "rehearsal" thus: "In the Hermitage theatre the audience even sat on cushions on the steps. The Sovereign came from Tsarskoe Selo with the Grand Duchesses, his daughters. Glazunov's music was magnificent, he beautifully projected the flogging of Christ. The Imperial orchestra played very well. After the performance, the Sovereign went backstage to talk with father... (he) was extremely excited, his face was dripping sweat, and he breathed heavily. When he played he performed a religious rite." It is of interest that several members of the House did not attend the performance, fearing the condemnation of the Synod, among then the Montenegrian sisters Militsa, and Stana. The Tsar, ambivalent as always, at the same time prohibited and praised the drama, which he had read to *dushka* Alix already in 1912. He sent a letter to his uncle-author as the following: "Dear Kostia!,.... your play made the deepest impression on me - more than once my eyes filled with tears, and I had a lump in my throat. I am certain that to see your play on stage and to hear the beautiful paraphrasing of what each of us knows from the Gospels, all this could but produce the most powerful effect on the spectator! It is for this reason that I share the opinion of the Holy Synod that it can not be publicly staged. With all my heart, your Nicky". (14, Sept, 1912) The Tsar was so fired by a hatred of the Jews, who crucified Christ, that he seemed to fear the possibility of a pogrom.

In 1883, at the age of twenty-five, the Grand Duke visited the homeland of his mother Altenburg, in the capacity of a representative of the House of Romanov, in order to attend the burial of his second cousin Margerita. There he met another second cousin, Princess Elizabeth, and they were attracted to each other at first sight. Their younger daughter, Princess Vera recalled that in her heart her mother always treasured the impression of a tall shapely young man with a reddish beard in a naval uniform, with beautiful hands, and long fingers (later he would be fond of wearing numerous rings), who stood leaning against a fireplace.

Against the will of her parents, who did not want their daughter to leave for Russia, Princess Elizabeth insisted on their engagement. The negotiations between the parents dragged on, but finally, a telegram was sent: "The piano has been bought." "Father came to Altenburg to make an official offer," recounted Princess Vera

Konstantinovna. "My mother remembered the sound of a sword, as father, in his Horse Guards' uniform mounted the staircase of the castle, heading to her parents." Later, when the year of engagement had run out, Konstantin described his confusion and spiritual alarm: "I love my fiancé," he wrote in his diary on the 11th of October, 1883, "without enthusiasm, without passion, without rapture, but I love her. " And again, also in October, "I am torn apart by fear. What if I don't like Elizabeth next time?"

K.R. was a fervently religious man; in time he wished to become the arch-procurator of the Synod, an ambition which his relatives regarded with more than a degree of humor. In contest to the majority of his relatives, he did not hunt, and never killed a living creature. And yet, since his youth when he had been introduced to "Sodomian Sin", his whole soul suffered because of his secret homosexuality the fact to become recently known after the publication of K.R.'s diaries. The entry of February 11, 1893 reads: "Again had to tell my confessor about the same sin as 14 years ago... Only thanks to Lord's unearned mercy, my sin remains a secret". Through a long period, he was plagued by shameful conscience, repentance, exhausting struggle; "the real attraction to my regiment is not military service, but being drawn to this or that soldier". The father of seven children, Konstantin is being tortured for fornication with bath-house attendants: "April

19,1904. My mind is in a bad way again, I am pursued by sinful thoughts, recollections and desires. I dream of going along to the bath-house on the Moika or to have the baths heated up at home, I can picture the familiar attendants, Alexei, Frolov, and particularly Sergei Syroezkin. My predilection has always been for simple men; I have neither sought, nor found partners in sin outside their circle. When passion speaks, the arguments of conscience, virtue, and reason are silenced". Same of September 12, 1904: "I sent for Yatsko... It was strange for me to hear him describe the familiar characteristics: he has never felt drawn to a woman, and has been infatuated with men several times. I did not confess to him that I knew these feelings from my own personal experience....He told me that, ever since the first time we met, his soul has been filled with rapturous feelings towards me, which grew all the time. How this reminds me of my own youth... he told me the names of people I had vaguely suspected of unnatural tendencies". Same of December 30, 1904: "Conscience and reason tell me I should forsake the path of indulgence once and for all, that is to say no longer to the bath-house, either at home or outside. But my feelings and my wild rebel - I want to see S. Syroezkin, whom I should not lead into temptation, since he is the first to wish it. That is the struggle. Lord help me. Will I free myself from sin, will I conquer myself, or will sin overcome me?"

The marriage of Their Highness took place in the church of the Winter Palace on the 15th of April, 1884, and the ceremony was conducted by the clergyman Yanyshev, the confessor of the Tsar's family. On the eve of the event, the traditional painstaking dressing of the bride and placing of the diamond crown took place in front of Empress Anna Ioannnovna's dressing table. Even after twenty years, on the 10th of April 1904, K.R. would recall his stupefaction and distress at that distant April time: "..my wife, then still a fiancé, arrived in Petersburg. It is painful and horrible to recall that she didn't want to kiss the cross."

On moving to the Marble Palace, where G. D. Konstantin and Grand Duchess Elizaveta Mavrikievna (1865 - 1927) settled following their marriage, they were met on the staircase by Alexandra Iosifovna and Konstantin Nikolaevich, in accordance with the tradition, with bread and salt, and they blessed them with an icon. In their own rooms on the ground floor of the southern wing, three of the most senior servants at his father's court brought them bread and salt on a silver salver sent by the Izmailov Regiment. The Emperor and Empress arrived for a family dinner.

The rooms of the young family, situated under the private apartments of Konstantin's mother, had maintained their eclectic character from the era of the architect Bruillov, though certain adjustments had been made prior to the sedding.

The portion of the building along the western facade remained entirely unchanged right up until 1886 when, as a result of the birth of their first child, Prince Ioann Konstantinovich of Imperial Blood, the service rooms of the lower floor were renovated and turned into nurseries. In 1886 and the following year, refurbishings were carried out according to the designs of the architect Anton K. Dzhiorghuli, who entered service at the Marble Palace after completing his studies at the Imperial Academy of Art. Independently, or together with the architect Zaitsev from Pavlosk, he completed the works within one construction season.

In accordance with Dzhiorghuli's plans, an autonomous interior ensemble in the Russian style was created, containing small rooms, or "khoromtsi", with service rooms, in the style of the the ancient Russian palaces of the XVIIth century. In all, twelve rooms were assigned for nursing the baby-prince Ioann, and those who followed next.

All the fireplaces, of the white Dutch tiles, and of painted Russian authentic tiles, were laid down by the master contractor Yefimov. Part of the interior was finished in oak: the ceiling and the walls in the entrance hall, the staircase banisters, the fancy folk design of the parquet the sills for the doors and windows, the frames, cupboards and shutters. The decorated fixtures of forged iron (catches, latches, hinges, locks, and door handles) were executed to the drawings of Dzjiorghuli, and included the exterior shutters for the windows with French glasses.

The furniture in the Old Russian style was made by the master joiner Feodorov. Several original items of Russian furniture, lamps and clocks were acquired in antique shops. Swaddle-tables were covered in suede, whilst morocco leather was used on the chairs and armchairs, and specially made linen curtains were hung on the windows.

The main entrance with a stone porch in the inner courtyard led to a small entrance hall with three oak glass-paneled doors, blue walls and a tiled fireplace in the style of a Moscow Tsars' rooms of the XVII century, with authentic green tiles and floral ornaments. The mural and ceiling painting, against a gold background, featured ornaments drawn from the religious books of the XVI century. The window casings were decorated with woven engravings, taking the iconostasis of St. Sophia of Novgorod as their model. The artistic furnishing of the entrance halls were completed with the portraits ('parsunas') of Tsar Mikhail Feodorovich and Tsarinas of the XVII century.

The main rooms were 'Gorenka' and 'Gulevaia'. The latter had a painted arched ceiling depicting Patriarch Filaret and the boyar Lukian Streshnev, and the boyar Lurian Steeshnev, praying on their knees together with Streshnev's daughter, Tsaritsa Evdokia Lukianovna. The window apertures went right to the level of the floor, and so their lower sections were protected by ironwork with colored glass shutters, the design of which was borrowed from the entrance doors of the Kremlin's Annunciation Cathedral. The furniture, chandeliers and candlesticks were manufactured according to Old Russian models. Judging by the description of 1886, only the German bronze clock with a lion and a Cupid were brought from the West.

Eight children grew up in the family, with six sons and two daughters: Ioann (1886), Gavriil (1887), Tatiana (1890), Konstantin (1891), Oleg (1892), Igor (1894) George (1903) and Vera (1906). Natalia, born in 1905, died three months after birth in her father's arms. Konstantin Konstantinovich was a strict father, and his children, for whom the words, "I don't want to", and "I can't" didn't extist, were rather afraid of him. In his study K.R. kept descriptions of all nine of his children's baptisms and wrote poems for each of their births.

Grand Duchess Elizabeth Mavrikievna ('Marva') did not adopt the Orthodox faith, remaining a Lutheran, which aroused grief and despair in her new relatives and her husband in particular. The children were, however, raised in the Orthodox faith. They read, served, and sang in the church choir. Ioann, who was particularly religious, had his own choir.

Everything Russian or national in the family

was regarded as Holy and was honored: the children had Russian names and Russian nannies. K.R. much disliked any foreign words in Russian speech, though his children studied foreign languages. In winter the children wore velvet coats similar to the kaftans of boyar-nobles, edged with sable, and sable hats topped in velvet. Money was never squandered: the coats were passed onto the next sibling as they were grown out of them. A coachman would convey them to the Tauride Garden for walks.

When K.R. was asked which of his sons was most like him, he replied that spiritually it was Ioann, and that as a poet it was Oleg. Grand Duke Konstantin managed to achieve the unachievable: Prince Oleg was allowed to study at the Imperial Lyceum, whereas all other offspring of the Romanovs were raised according to ancient traditions, which included training in military institutes and service in the army.

Every morning the children would go to greet their parents on the ground floor, through a small vestibule with a marble staircase and a candelabra of dark bronze: a flying Mercury holding a candlestick, with one leg rested on the head of Cupid, personifying the wind. In the reception room the walls were covered in carved panels, whilst the upper sections of the walls were covered in printed gilded wallpaper with a pattern formed from flowers, vines, and birds. In front of the brown tiled corner fireplace with its majolica

frieze there lay a polar bear rug. On the wall hung
A. Kuindzhi's painting, "*Night over the Dnieper.*"
K.R. had bought it as a young naval officer in the
artist's own studio, where he had been brought by
Ivan Turgenev. At first Kuindzhi had said that the
painting "is not for you, young man," as he hadn't
recognized the Grand Duke. Konstantin,
nevertheless, acquired the painting and took it
with him on his voyage on the *Duke of Edinburgh*
frigate. Artistic society and the artist himself
were horrified, believing that the famous picture
might be ruined on the voyage, though it survived
unharmed.

Nearby in the prayer room, icons were hung,
and an icon-lamp was permanently burning.
Every day, from the large family church, a new
icon was brought of that saint whose holy name-
day was being celebrated. After having prayed,
Konstantin would greet his children and go to the
dining room, to have tea with his wife, and read
the newspapers. Half the wall space of the dining
room was taken by a picture by the artist
Sedestrem: the Guards carry the dead Swedish
King Charles XII on a stretcher. "The decor of his
rooms lack style" wrote G.D. Andrei Vladimirovich
in his diary in 1915, "but all the objects, in their
selection, explain the mood of this outstanding
man."

In the musical drawing room (the Gothic
room) the master of the house would play the
piano daily. In the next drawing room the

monogram K and E could be found above the windows. The multi-colored painted ceiling depicted Apollo, Athene, and a female figure holding a lyre. The coved ceiling shows a date: completed in 1894 by the artist Lipghart. From 1900 on a marble bust of Ophelia stood in the drawing room, a present from Elizabeth to her husband on the anniversary of the day when he first played Hamlet.

In K.R.'s working study the suite of furniture was in mahogany, in the "Jacob" style. Above carved wall panels, there was a leather section with a printed pattern of a griffin, from the coat-of-arms of the Romanovs. An interesting description of the study is contained in K.R.'s diary dated 16th of March, 1887: "How wonderful my study looks! The pictures are hung, and directly in front of me there is a *Pieta* of the Italian school of the XVIth century. To the right, in the recess there is a copy by Sokolov with Bellini's Madonna, on which I wrote a poem in '82, and words are engraved into the frame. Further to the right... hangs a picture of Lombardian school - *Christ as a boy*, - to the right...two Flemmish pictures: *Mother* by Gherard Poe, he himself painted it, and a little lower, there's a *Man's head...*" Here K.R. wrote and kept his comprehensive archive in perfect order, he regularly entered his diary, with a stipulation in his will that it shouldn't be published for ninety years. According to K.R.'s will, his copious correspondence was to be returned to the individuals who wrote them. He bequeathed Puskin's ring with its huge emerald to the Academy of Sciences, which had once been given to him for eternal keeping by the daughter of Vladimir Dal[1].

And so, life continued: family, service, theatre, poetry. His military career continued unabated. In 1891, G.D. Konstantin was transferred from the Izmailovsky Regiment to be commander of the Preobrazhensky, where the heir apparent to the throne was to serve under his command. As mentioned earlier, K.R. had noted in his diary in 1888: "My life and my activities are entirely fixed…. For others I am a soldier. For myself, I am a poet. That is my true calling."

A decree of Alexander III, in 1889, appointed Konstantin the President of the Academy of Sciences, thus numerous academics became frequent guests at the Marble Palace. The Grand Duke supported the research work of Ivan Pavlov in physiology and stood up for the eminent chemist Dimitri Mendeleyev, who many did not want in the Academy. K.R. headed the sobriety society, donating large sums for the treatment of those that had lost their way. He founded the Imperial Women's Pedagogical Institute in the Petrogradsky district, which was distinguished by the high professional standards of its teachers. Directly adjacent to the Institute, a grammar school was built at the Grand Duke's expense and bore his name. In the Education Commission he fought against Pobedonostsev for village schools to be set up to counterweight the church parish schools. He opened a Sunday School at the Marble Palace for deprived children. He was a uniquely many-sided, active individual, overflowing with goodness.

Baroness Sophie Buxhouveden recalled that "the evening receptions at the Grand Duke's reflected his broad outlook. Gray haired academics sat together with the composer Kui, famous singers and actors, Preobrazhenskhy officers with their wives, along with the Headmistress of the Ladies' Courses Ms. Babkova and Captain Kolchak, a famous and brilliant researcher in those days. The host was kind and attentive to all. He was meeting his guests at the foot of the staircase in the vestibule and accompanied them, giving his arm to every woman, be it a princess or a teacher, into the main rooms."

In 1992, Princess Vera Konstantinovna recounted an amusing story to this author. She told of a certain passerby, who entered the palace to give a piece of advice: tell the Grand Duke that he shouldn't totally undress himself, as he could be seen standing naked through the window of the ground floor. It became apparent that the poor man had mistaken "Saint Sebastian" for the master of the Marble Palace.

One of K.R.'s last appointments in 1900 was

that of General-Inspector of the military cadets schools of Russia. He had a genuine love for his charges, understanding their woes and joys and giving support and guidance. His wonderful memory for faces helped him to not only remember their names, but even their nicknames, which he would often invent himself. In the event of his having forgotten a name he would rest his arm on the cadet's head, and ask him to remind him of the first letter. The cadets adored their chief, and their parents had every reason to be grateful to him: he fought against the *tsukanye*[1], introduced parents' days and was always available. Far from the world of politics, K.R. remained a monarchist, loyal to the Tsar and a supporter of aristocracy.

In 1905, K.R. lived for the most part in Pavlovsk, only making visits to the Marble Palace and the family would gather with greater infrequency. The ranks of the family continued to be filled. In summer, 1911, two weddings were celebrated in Pavlovsk: Prince Ioann married Princess Yelena Petrovna of Serbia, and they had a son and a daughter. Two months later, Tatiana married Prince Konstantin Bagration-Mukhranski. The Marble Palace was perpetually being renovated to accommodate the growing children.

One cannot dismiss K.R.'s great effort in preservation of such a pearl of art and architecture as the Pavlovsk estate. "Although after my father's death Pavlovsk became my property by right of primogeniture (Nicola was deprived of that right), I did not feel a full landowner. All accounts have been signed by Mama as well, and , though not being an owner of Pavlovsk, she was certainly not estranged by me from the rights she had enjoyed during Papa's illness", he recalled in a diary, entry of October 8, 1896. Konstantin devoted himself with the greatest care to restoring every object to the original place it occupied in the days of Empress Maria. He used a detailed inventory, drawn up by the first owness herself, and provided for a thorough restoration of the interior.

The Grand Duke worshipped his Pavlovsk. He learned the story of each and every bush, and pathway, and delighted in talking about them. Probably more than any other suburb of Petersburg, Pavlovsk retained the character of "sophisticated olden times". When caring for his estate, the Grand Duke occasionally went to extremes. To this day, they use karsel lamps at Pavlovsk Palace, there is no electric power", Baron Driesen wrote in December, 1916

In the summer of 1914, the Grand Duke and his wife were in Germany, where Konstantin was undergoing a cure. They disbelieved the rumours of an impending war. A telegram from his brother Dmitri informed him of the events in Sarajevo. Collecting his wife, Georgie and Vera from his father-in-law, he wanted to start promptly for

Russia. In the conditions of anti-Russian hysteria their journey was no easy matter.

The Germans would have interned him, unless his wife Mavra used her connections with the German Empress. After much parley they were allowed to depart. Their homeward train stopped many a time, they were finally "unloaded", and literally at gunpoint, they had to proceed on foot, and managed to cross the border where a Cossack unit found them in a ditch by the edge of a road. The adjutant, Prince Shakhovskoi, showed the Grand Duke's visiting card to the officer, who spent a long time trying to work out how such a prestigious person had managed to turn up in a ditch on the Prussian border on the first day of the war. But he recognized his commander, who he had seen only a year before at his military academy.

The family made their way to Pavlovsk, the Marble Palace having been converted into a field hospital. The older sons had already set off to war. In October of 1914, the horrifying news of Prince Oleg being mortally wounded during a cavalry charge reached them. The parents set off for Vilna, where they reached their dying son. They brought with them the St. George's Cross of his grandfather. Prince Oleg died twenty minutes later in their arms. The death of the son, a budding poet and artist, was not only a shock, but also hastened the demise of the Grand Duke.

Konstantin Konstantinovich died in his study

in Pavlovsk on the 2nd of June, 1915, of angina pectoris. He was buried at the grand ducal mausoleum of St. Peter and Paul's. The streets were lined with cadets, accompanying the hearse that carried the body of their mentor, as he went on his last journey. It was the last state burial to take place in the House of Romanov. The old valet Fokin, who had stayed on with the Grand Duke from the Russo-Turkish war, brought a little box, which he had unfailingly taken on all their trips, filled with soil from Strelna, the birthplace of G.D. Konstantin, and this soil was spread on the coffin top. The lid bore an engraving in the Grand Duchess's hand-writing, the lines from Lermontov: "How can one ever forget the homeland?"

And so, in the first year of World War I, the family had lost three of its dearest members: the third was the husband of Princess Tatiana, Prince Konstantin Bagration Mukhranski, who was killed near Lvov in May of 1915. His widow was left with two little children, Teymuraz, and Natalia. But the family could have had no idea how merciful Providence had been in taking the father two years before the outbreak of the Revolution. Of Konstantin Konstantinovich's eight children, only four, Gavriil, George, Tatiana, and Vera would survive the war and the revolution.

In 1917 the family resided in the Marble Palace, in close proximity to the events of the October coup. In 1918 the Grand Duchess secretly sold her jewels and outfits, in order not to die of starvation. On occasion affluent buyers would visit the impoverished family: a marvelous album commemorating the coronation of Alexander II went to a Muscovite merchant.

In 1915, Prince Ioann and Princess Elena became the last legal owners of Pavlovsk where they lived until 1917. Disaster came in March 1917. G.D. Ksenia wrote in her diary "at night, a crowd of soldiers and similar riff-raff with machine-guns rushed in, and they demanded that they be given arms. [Mar. Nik] Baulina met them and asked them to leave and not to make so much noise so as not to scare "Her Majesty" "And who's Her Majesty?" - "The Queen of Greece". "We don't need any Greek Queen" and they left, but they robbed Elena P. stealing her valuable things which hadn't been put away , . . . "and boots and warm clothes of the children - Terrible - what a disgrace." Soon the palace was expropriated.

In mid-March, 1918, according to a decree of the Petrograd Cheka, all Romanovs were required to present themselves at the Cheka in three days, and give a written obligation not to leave. In the end of March, three young Konstantinovichi - Ioann, Konstantin and Igor - were deported from Petrograd to Viatka. They were transferred to the Urals, where they lived under arrest in a "field school house," in Alapayevsk of Perm gubernia, together with Grand Duchess Elizabeth

Feodorovna (Ella), a nun at that time, G.D. Sergei Mikhailovich, and Prince Vladimir Palay, until the late night of 17/18 of July, when all captives were thrown alive to an abandoned mineshaft near Alapayevsk. There they died of their wounds and thirst.

Not long before his arrest, the very pious Ioann became a subdeacon; he wanted to become a priest, but it was too late. His wife Elena followed him into exile, was arrested in Ekaterinburg and kept prisoner in several places. Psychologically broken, the captive was brought to Moscow, under Cheka control.

As late as December, 1918, Elena was released due to the petitioning of a Norwegian attaché, and thus she left Russia for good. As if to protect her injured soul after the utterly devastating experience, the last mistress of Pavlovsk forbade her two children to speak the Russian language.

In the summer of 1918, Grand Duchess Elizabeth Mavrikievna, with Georgie and Vera moved from their palace to the Zherebtsov's house on the Palace Embankment ("just good people," Princess Vera told the author in 1991). Prince Gavriil, who was ill, managed to leave for Finland with his morganatic wife Antonina Nesterovskaya, a former ballerina who sought assistance from the Commissar for the Theatres, Maria Andreyeva, who was in turn the wife of Maxim Gorky. The Greek Queen Olga managed to leave by train after the Danish diplomatic mission had given its support to her cause. In October of 1918, having received permission with difficulty, Elizabeth Mavrikievna sailed aboard the Swedish ship with Georgie, Vera and two grandchildren. The Grand Duchess died in Leipzig in 1927.

Of the Konstantinovichi borne before 1917 Princess Vera Konstantinovna, died on 11 January, 2001 at the Tolstoy Foundation located at Valley Cottage, New York. Her sister Princess Ekaterina Ioannovna who lived in Uruguay, died in Montevideo on 13 March 2007.

And what of the splendid palace, that center of culture and intellect? It was plundered, as were the majority of palaces between 1918 and 1920, when any form of security was effectively nonexistent. The smaller items were stolen; the larger valuables that were left were included in an inventory of the 13th of May, 1920 which comprised several folders. A special commission on the material cultural history, which was attached to the Academy of Sciences, took control of the premises and property of the Marble Palace as listed in the inventory. Great scientist-linguist N.Y. Marr signed the inventory of behalf of the academy, the other parties signing being the watchmen Feodorov and the housekeeper Slepkin, one of them leaving a cross instead of a signature.

During the first years of the Soviet power, the Marble Palace housed a museum reflecting poor and decadent ways of life. For a period of about fifteen years, valuables were passed on through different institutions, from owner to owner, the number remaining falling sharply. The church and table silverware were sold at auction, what's more, according to their weight. The paintings and books were spread through various museums and various fortuitous individuals.

In 1937 the V.I.Lenin Museum opened in the Marble Palace. Shortly before a hurried program of works was undertaken to remove any traces of Gothic, "Russian" or other styles on the premises. The Palace became "simple, like Lenin." Not daring to wholly destroy the legacy of Rinaldi, and Bruillov, the renovators tore down the wall and recesses, plastered over the rich murals, and covered the decorative parquet with synthetic materials.

The Lenin Museum no longer exists. There is now hope for the rebirth of the invanquishable beauty of the palace. Having awoken from a historical hopeless slumber, the present day Russians have finally put up a gravestone in the burial vault of the grand ducal mausoleum, in the Peter and Paul Fortress, over the resting place of a great son of Russia, a wonderful poet, the founder of Pushkin House (IRLI, The Institute of Russian Literature), and the President of the Academy of Sciences - Grand Duke Konstantin Konstantinovich.

Konstantin Konstantinovich as Mozart, 1880

Grand Duke Konstantin Konstantinovich
as Hamlet on 21st February 1899

Grand Duke Konstantin Konstantinovich dressed in
17th century costume in February 1903

Konstantin Konstantinovich as Don Cesar
in the play 'Bride of Messina'. 1909

Grand Duke Konstantin Konstantinovich as Joseph
of Arimathea in the drama "King of the Jews". 1914

Prince Gabriel Konstantinovich in exile
Circa 1940s

- III -

Memories of My Father

by Prince Gabriel Konstantinovich
Translated by Nina Toulina

I can see my father's image standing before my eyes. He was tall with a light tiny beard, very fine hands, with long fingers all in rings. When he greeted his children, he kissed us by taking our faces in his large hands. On communion day before going to the church he did not kiss us because it is not permitted until after having received communion. And only then did he greet us by shaking our hands.

At eight o'clock in the morning when my father used to come to the dining room to have his coffee he would send his valet for us. Our nurses—Vava and Atja—would take us to father. Usually we found father wearing a grey double-breasted jacket and seated in the corner on the sofa at a small table on a raised place.

In the dining room there was a huge painting by Seiderstrem depicting King Charles XII of Sweden on a stretcher being carried by his guards. My father liked this painting very much. At the Marble Palace in his reception study room among others there was a picture painted by

Kuindzhe, *The Night on the Dnieper River*. My father bought it when he was a young naval officer. He liked it and wanted to purchase it. But Kuindzhe answered: "Young man, it's not for you." He didn't recognize my father. Still the picture was purchased by him. And when departing out for sea he wanted to take it with him. When Kuindzhe was advised of this he was going to bring legal action against my father because he feared that his famous picture would be lost at sea. Still my father took it, nothing happened to it and there was no legal action taken against him.

In the evening when we, children, went to bed, Papa and Mama came to us in order to be present as we said our evening prayers. At first my elder brother Ioanchik and then I kneeled in front of the icon-case in our bedroom and said our prayers, among them was *Guardian Angel* which according to family legend was said by Emperor Alexander II when he was a child.

My father demanded that we know the anthems for all the major festivals by heart and to say them on the designated days. Quite often my uncle—*Djadenka*—papa's younger brother—Grand Duke Dimitri Constantinovich—was present at our evening prayers. When we made mistakes our parents and Djadenka corrected us.

My father was very strict with us and we were afraid of him. Such words as "I can't" or "I don't want to" did not exist for us. He nurtured our independence: we had to do everything ourselves, to keep our toys in order, to put them in their places. My father hated foreign words inserted into the Russian language. He wanted Russian to be our first language. That is the reason why our nurses were Russian and everything in our home was made in the Russian manner.

At the Marble Palace in father's chapel on the way from his study to the corridor there were many icons hanging and always an icon lamp glimmering. Every day the icon of that particular Saint's day was brought from the palace church to my father's chapel. Such icons, all in one style were presented to my father by my uncles—the Grand Dukes Serge Alexandrovich and Paul Alexandrovich.

Later when we were older and were able to go to greet our father on our own, the valet on duty occasionally asked us to wait outside quietly. "Your father is praying"—he used to say. After praying our father greeted us, went to the dining room, where he had his coffee, and looked through the morning newspaper which was waiting for him.

Whether in Petersburg, Pavlovsk or in Strelna when father had free time he went for a walk. We enjoyed those outings with our father. Our mother often joined us.

Sometimes at home our father sat down at the piano. He played the piano extremely well. He had had an excellent musical education. He was taught by Rudolf Vasilievich Kjundinger whom my father called—"Rudi". Kjundinger came once a week to the palace and my father played the piano under his supervision in the "gothic" room. Afterwards Rudi always stayed behind to have breakfast. My father had a marvellous touch. While playing the piano he was especially good when he was playing Chopin's preludes. I enjoyed listening to his playing and looking at his handsome fingers running upon the keyboard.

My father had a passion for both reading and writing. He attentively kept up with all the latest Russian and foreign literature. He tried to read all the latest books. Throughout his life he kept a diary which he wrote in copybooks with yellow leather covers. He bequeathed these diaries to be published 90 years after his death.

In the evening after dinner with a cigar in his mouth my father used to seat himself again at his writing desk. His small cosy study always had the pleasant smell of cigars. He did not like to discuss business affairs in the presence of his family especially his own personal problems. When he had any problems he suffered silently, "kept them in his heart", —that's the reason his heart was so weak.

Thinking back over those many years I recall my father's life like that but I must admit his life went far beyond that of his family limits. His principle life interests were outside our palace. He belonged to Russia.

He was a combatant chief who in a fatherly

manner took care of his soldiers. He knew all of the non-commissioned officers surnames first of the Izmailovsky and then of the Preobragensky regiments.

He was the head chief and then general-inspector of military educational establishments who many times travelled throughout Russia visiting hospitals and military schools.

He actively participated in the work of the Sobriety Committee trying to put Russia on the road to good health.

He was a distinguished statesman and reformer at the Literacy Committee whose goal was to make all Russians literate, at least able to read and write. He also fought against Pobedonoscev for opening public schools.

He was the founder and actually the Head of the Petersburg Female Teachers' Training College.

He was the enemy of student persecution.

For many years he was President of the Academy of Sciences where his name is linked to so many important personal undertakings.

He was the creator of the Belles-Lettres Literature Branch at the Academy and he himself was its first freely elected honorary academician.

He was the organizer of the once widely known "dosugi" which organized and hosted leisure activities for the Izmaylovsky Regiment.

He was the chairman of The Russian Musical Society and corresponded with many prominent musicians, in particular with Tchaikovsky.

And at last he was a well-known literary figure, widely acknowledged by all—as the poet K.R.—who left not only a rich literary heritage—which included his original works—but also his translations of Goethe's *Ithigenia in Tavrida*, Shiller's *Bride of Messina*, and Shakespeare's *Hamlet*. He himself was the embodiment of those great performances on the stage. He also left his valuable comments upon these world-famous treasures. And at the end of his life he created the drama, *King of Judea* where as its acknowledged by all, he united a deep religious feeling and exquisite representative gift. Through all his versatile activities he showed a feverish energy and desire to oversee his projects from beginning to the very end.

My father was the second son of the naval general Grand Duke Constantine Nikolayevich. He was born in 1858 and since his childhood had been prepared for the naval service. But the naval service was not for him and at the same time his poor health would not allow him to continue to serve. Therefore, he left the naval service for the army.

As an infantryman he wanted to serve in the Pavlovsky Life Guards Regiment but my grandfather demanded that he join the Izmaylovsky Regiment because my father's name had been recorded on the list of the Izmaylovsky Regiment from the time of his birth. So on the 15th of December, 1883 he became an *izmaylovets*. Being a lover of poetry and drama he organised the so called "Dosugi" which means "our leisure time" at the Izmaylovsky Regiment. These literary gatherings prepared amateur performances for the stage. Shakespeare's *Hamlet* was staged at the Hermitage Theatre in February 1900. I remember that performance evening quite well. After father left for the theatre (he performed the main part of Hamlet) our man-servant lackey Krjukov hardly managed to convey a heavy marble bust of Ofelia to my parents drawing room. That was mother's present to my father. She wanted father to see it at once when he returned from his performance.

At the officers gatherings of the Izmaylovsky Regiment, theatre performances took place on a folding stage which was a gift from Davidoff, a prominent actor of the Alexandrinsky Theatre. Almost all performances of *Dosugi* were produced by Davidoff.

On the 22nd of April 1891 my father was appointed as Commander of the Preobragensky Life Guards Regiment. He was at the head of that regiment till March 1900. During that period for some time the first battalion commander was the Heir-Tsesarevich Nicholas Alexandrovich (the future Emperor Nikolai II) before ascending the throne. According to the popular opinion he was a zealous and efficient officer.

When my father came into position as the regiment commander he tried to improve the soldiers living conditions from the first days of their arrival to the regiment. He would quite often invite the officers sometimes with their wives to the palace for breakfast or dinner. I remember once after such a dinner one of those ladies taught my mother to dance *pas de quatre* which was very much in fashion in those days.

I enjoyed watching my father riding in front of his regiment. Riding in line service he looked so elegant and handsome sitting on horseback. In spring, the regiment left for Krasnoe Selo and remained there from April till August. The whole week he spent at the camp and came to Pavlovsk or Strelna only on Saturday evenings. He came in a carriage led by three horses. They were always driven by a coachman by the name of Philipp who served my father from the day of the Emperor Alexander III's coronation.

We loved to visit our father in Krasnoe Selo in a landau of our own pulled by four post-chaise horses and returned back the same day. We drank tea at our father's place, walked about the camp, looked in at the stables, mounted his grey vaulting horse Maruska as his groom Piter Zazdravnji held it steady by the bridle. Once we returned to the camp when the regiment had just returned from manoeuvres. The regiment formed up in front of the first line, our father mounted on his horseback commanded: *"pod znamija, slushay, na kara'ul",* (which means — "in the name of the standard, listen to, present arms") the music started to play the regiment march, the banner was taken away. It was so solemn that I went into raptures.

Once our aunt—*Tetja* Olia (the Queen of Greece—Olga Constantinovna) came to the camp with us. I remember we were going somewhere and happened to be on the Krasnoselskoe Highway. At that time Grand Duke Vladimir Alexandrovich and Prince Obolensky who was Guards corps commander were driving along the highway. When Vladimir Alexandrovich saw Tetja Olia he stopped the carriage, got out, kneeled on one leg before her and kissed her hand. He always enjoyed such jokes.

In 1900 my father was appointed to the post of the head commander of military educational establishments. That was to be a new fruitful period of his life. Embarking on a new and extremely responsible career, my father following the directions of his heart and intellect, set a clear task before himself: first of all, in military students to meet the children who decided to devote their talents to serving the throne and Motherland, to meet the children who needed not only strictness but also moral support, father's cordial advise and favourable instructions. It was necessary to reject severe formal relations and to form a close bond with them. And he did just that. During the fifteen years when he was the head of military educational establishments he visited all the cadet corps and colleges scattered throughout

Russia.

Due to his excellent memory my father easily memorized each of the cadets surnames. If when out walking and he met a cadet at once he addressed him by his surname followed by his first name. And it was seldom that he made a mistake. The cadets loved and respected him and up to this day they honour his memory with reverence. In Paris after emigration a former cadet—Mohammedan—showed me a copy of the Koran which my father had presented him when he learned that the cadet had not read the Koran. He said: "What Mohammedan are you if you do not read the Koran!". That cadet so much appreciated father's gift that he even took it when he left the Motherland for ever.

Much of my father's poetic legacy is still in unpublished manuscripts. I have found references about it in his correspondence with his sister where he frankly spoke about his "creative torments" and where a number of pages were full with never published or other variants of already published poetry.

He never spoke to us children about his literary work. In general he spoke little to us and never shared his literary impressions. I must admit it was our fault because not one of us other than my brother Oleg who heroically perished in 1914 was interested in literature. It is very likely that father was closer to him, as they seemed to understood each other.

When poetic moods captivated my father he forgot about his surroundings and concentrated only about his verses. He used to arrive at the Academy of Sciences building where he was the president or to the Chief Administration building of military educational establishments and remained in the carriage not getting out. His thoughts were preoccupied with the poetry world. The coachman Foma used to say to him then: "Your Imperial Highness, we have arrived": My father returned to reality and got out of the carriage.

The consummation of all my father's creative work became his drama *King of Judea* about the earthly life of Jesus Christ. The Holy Synod was against the staging of this lofty drama in which Jesus Christ himself never appeared. We believe that the idea for the drama had been suggested by Tchaikovsky, who in October 1889 wrote to my father about this gospel theme.

My father's death and funeral

On the following day, Diadenka sent me to the Emperor at Tsarskoe Selo to ask instructions concerning how to dress my father – a full-dress uniform or a jacket with a high collar? My father had requested to bury him dressed in the 15th Grenadier regimentals. Arriving at the Alexander Palace I asked to be received by the Emperor. He received me in his study and instructed me to dress father in a jacket with a high collar.

From the Emperor I went to the Grand Marshal of the Court – Count Benckendorff, also at Djadenka's request. I asked instructions whether to put the Saint George Cross on. Benckedorff said not to put it on. Count Benckendorff lived in the Great Palace at Tsarskoe Selo in the so called Lyceum wing where the Imperial Alexandrovskiy Lyceum had been housed when originally founded and where Pushkin lived as a student.

My father was embalmed in the Mezzanine Room, next to the former study of the Emperor Paul. I believe it was his valet's room in former days. The doctors found a sore on father's heart. Now my father's words that he had felt "heart wounds" now made sense. But he complained of his suffering very seldom, preferring to conceal it all inside.

After one of the services for the dead in father's study, Djadenka, my brothers and I, also our court officials placed our father in the coffin. The coffin was taken upstairs to the magnificent rotunda on the first floor. Exactly a year   before in that very room, my parents had hosted a gala Family dinner in honour of the King of Saxony who was visiting Petersburg at the time.

At the coffin head there were placed three flags: the admiral, the vice-admiral, and the rear admiral because my father was on the list of the Guards crew. On both sides of the coffin there stood representatives of the military educational establishments and also of the units where my father was on the list.

Unfortunately father's body had been poorly embalmed and as a result his facial expression had changed greatly. The body was covered with a golden brocade bedspread edged with ermine. There were chandeliers with candles lit all around the coffin. The situation was very solemn. During one of the services for the dead a life guard standing as a sentry with a riffle on his shoulder near the coffin fainted.

Many people came to the services for the dead. The Family was standing in the rotunda itself and the public was standing near by - in the Greek Room and even on the staircase landing.

The removal of the coffin from Pavlovsk Palace and the journey to the Peter and Paul's Fortress in Petrograd took place on the 8th day after father's death. The removal took place after lunch at about three o'clock. The Emperor, Paul Alexandrovich and George Mikhailovich came. Other Family members met father's body at the Tsar's branch of the Tsarskoe Selo station in Petrograd. The Emperor followed the coffin through the palace courtyard and then left for Tsarskoe Selo. But all the rest took the coffin off up to the Pavlovsk railway station and together with it went to Petrograd by a special train.

Many people stood along the highway by which the coffin was taken up to Pavlovsk. As we were approaching the vauxhall on foot, the railway station orchestra which usually gave concerts at the railway station, began to play a funeral march.

Our train arrived at the Tsar's branch platform in Petrograd. The meeting was prepared there. The Emperor together with the two Empresses stood on the platform. The Empresses were dressed in black crape mourning dresses with Saint Andrew ribbons. The coffin was taken out of the rail car and put on a gun-carriage of the Constantinovskiy Artillery College where my father was on the list to the sounds of "Kol Slaven!". The College cadets served as drivers. Pages with torches in their hands went on foot on both sides of the coffin.

The Empresses and Grand Duchesses went by gala mourning carriages. My mother and nine-year-old Vera went in the carriage with the Empress Alexandra Fedorovna. The troops were lined up all our sad way. Ioanchik and I went on foot on both sides of Djadenka.

The next day, a burial service for the dead followed by a funeral ceremony took place in the Peter and Paul Fortress. The coffin was elevated under a canopy. All around there were guards standing. The British Ambassador Buchanan was standing to the right of the Family next to Grand Duke George Mikhailovich.

My mother remained quiet and as always

with great dignity. When the coffin lid was slowly lowered down, my mother was bending lower and lower to see his dead face up to the very last moment.

My father was buried in the new sepulchre where my grand father, grand mother and my sister Natala had also been buried. The coffin was lowered into a very deep and narrow grave. Thank God, father's valet Fockin, who had served him since the Russo-Turkish war recollected that my father had always carried a little box with him which contained some soil from Strelna where he was born. He had brought that box with him to the sepulchre and spread the earth on the coffin lid when it was lowered down. Lermontov's words were engraved on the box's metal cover in mother's handwriting: "How can we not remember our Motherland?"

The grave was sealed with a marble slab similar to those on the other graves. Before my father's funeral, I did not know that the coffins are lowered in such deep and narrow graves. The tomb slabs are placed on the stone floor level. Before, all the members of the Romanov Dynasty were buried inside the Peter's and Paul's Cathedral. A tall, white marble sarcophagi with a gold cross was placed above each grave. It was possible to kneel in front of the sarcophagus, to lean against it and to pray. This way one could feel close to the dearly departed. And in the new sepulchre the dead who were dear to you were somewhere under your feet. How can the person coming to pray feel close to them?

Seldom in life can one meet so good a person as my father. Almost 40 years have passed since his death. His unforgettable image stands before my eyes as if he were still alive. I feel I need him, I feel lost without him. Sometimes I'd like nothing more than to go to my father and to have a heart-to-heart talk with him.

Grand Duke Konstantin Konstantinovich, Empress Alexandra Feodorovna, Emperor Nicholas II and Grand Duchess Elizaveta Mavrikievna. Konstantin Palace, Strelna.

Grand Duke Konstantin Konstantinovich and his wife Grand Duchess Elizaveta Mavrikievna, were among the relatively few Romanovs on intimate terms with Nicholas II and Alexandra Feodorovna, who found Konstanin's devotion to his family a welcome respite from the playboy lifestyle of many of the other Grand Dukes.

Her Highness Princess Vera Konstantinovna, seated in front of a portrait of her beloved father, in her apartment at the Tolstoy Foundation, Valley Cottage, NY. 1988

Memories of My Father

by Princess Vera Konstantinovna
Translated by Irene W. Galaktionova

The name of my father, the Grand Duke Konstantin Konstantinovich, will live in history. The time will undoubtedly come when his life and activity, both as statesman and as a man of letters, will find their biographer. In this brief address I cannot hope to even remotely cover so big and important a subject. All I can do now is touch on the main landmarks of my father's flamboyant and memorable life path - but at least I can share some more personal memories and details of our family life which are unlikely to ever end up on the pages of history at large.

My father was born in 1858 into the family of Grand Duke Konstantin Nikolaevich and Grand Duchess Alexandra Iosifovna, born Princess of Saxe Altenburg.

The name of my grandfather, the Grand Duke Konstantin Nikolaevich, a man of excellent education and the widest intellectual horizons, is closely associated with the reforms carried out by Alexander II "the Liberator" and especially the historic emancipation of serfs of which my grandfather was a most passionate supporter. He was one of the main figures in the stellar entourage of statesmen surrounding Alexander II. He was, in chronological order: Viceroy of the Kingdom of Poland, President of the Council of State and Admiral-General of the Imperial Navy. Duly reformed thanks to my grandfather's tireless activity, the Russian fleet was able to take its place among the world's leading seafaring nations. His vigorous and passionate nature made my grandfather one of the most memorable and vivid personalities of Alexander II's reign.

My grandmother was a perfect match for him. The Grand Duchess Alexandra Iosifovna was well-known in her day for her exceptional beauty, her lively and prodigious mind and rare sense of humour.

It was no surprise that my father's parental home with its abundance of intellectual and cultural interests proved to be a highly fertile soil in which to nurture and develop his natural talents.

He had revealed his aptitude for the written word already at an early age, as well as that for poetry, music and theatre. Together with his father he played in the orchestra conducted by the great Johann Strauss himself. He often took part in amateur dramatical productions. He played the piano remarkably well with an exceptional feeling and wrote several short pieces for that instrument.

As the son of an Admiral General, he

entered the Navy, following both the family tradition and his father's desire. For his courage and bravery during the 1877-1878 Black Sea campaign he received the Cross of St. George 4th class. In 1876 he joined the Grand Duke Alexey Alexandrovich's delegation to the United States, visiting New York on the frigate *Svetlana* as part of the Russian squadron.

Still, naval service proved too much for his fragile health. Father was never particularly robust. Much to his own father's displeasure and even anger, he left the Navy to serve as a squadron commander in the elite Izmaylovsky regiment of the Imperial Russian Guard.

In 1883, my father finally seized the chance to visit his mother's home town of Altenburg, the capital of the Duchy of Saxe-Altenburg. He went there to represent his family at the funeral of his second cousin Margarethe who had died of pneumonia at fourteen years of age. There he met another member of the family - Elizabeth, the late girl's elder sister. This encounter proved to be life-changing. The two second cousins liked each other at first sight. I remember my mother telling me about the impression my father had made on her when they first met. He was standing leaning against a mantelpiece in the Naval uniform that suited him so well. When they sat next to each other at the dinner table, my father studied the silver bracelet mounted with a colourless stone that his future fiancée was wearing. He asked her,

"Do you like the shape of this bracelet?" She answered in the affirmative. "When I have a fiancée, I'll give her one exactly like yours," he said to her. And that's exactly what he did do later when they became engaged. I inherited the bracelet after my mother's death and I still wear it all the time.

My mother's parents weren't at all happy about her moving to Russia which they viewed as a country of constant uprisings and revolutions. Still, their daughter, usually so obedient and docile, declared that she "wasn't scared of gunpowder!" The negotiations took a long time until finally, a coded telegram was sent to Russia, announcing that "the piano had been sold".

Their wedding was in 1884. Now my father's life and happiness were complete. He shared his time between his family, military service and poetry. He loved his regiment dearly, founding Izmaylovsky Pastimes, the first literary society - something previously unheard-of in military circles! This allowed officers to discuss the newest additions to Russian poetry and fiction, including readings from a guest star poet Apollon Nikolaevich Maykov.

He was then promoted from his post as company commander, bypassing the rank of battalion commander, to become commander of the Preobrazhensky Regiment of Lifeguards.

In 1899, by Imperial decree my father was entrusted with the responsible mission of preparing a new military cadre. He received the post of first Chief, then later Inspector General of Military Colleges. All of you know full well what a lucky choice it was and to what heights my father brought the Cadet Corps and cadet schools. We all know about his sincere devotion to his protégés and the sincere interest he took in their problems, pastimes and personal lives, their joys and sorrows. He had an exceptional memory for names and faces, even the cadets' nicknames that he sometimes bestowed on them himself. He knew and remembered personally a multitude of cadets and junkers.

You could publish a large volume of cadets' memoirs about my father. I'd have loved so much to see such a collection appear in print to mark his upcoming centenary in 1958.

The cadets loved their chief to bits. The following incident may serve as an example of their affection and trust in him. A certain cadet Sereda was expelled from two of the corps, Poltavsky and Voronezhsky - as cadets used to joke, for his "quiet successes and loud behaviour". He decided to appeal to my father and went all the way to Pavlovsk. Our doorman wouldn't allow him in. Without hesitation, this ingenious young man walked around the park and climbed a tree to do some preliminary reconnaissance. Seeing my father working in his study, he entered it. My father heard a slight noise and raised his head from his work.

"Sereda? What are you doing here?" he asked, immediately recognising the boy.

The boy answered with a nervous stutter, "Yo-our Royal High-ighness, they've chucked me out!"

"Very well," Father said. "So have you decided what you're going to do now?"

To which the boy exclaimed without hesitation, "Your Roya-yal Hi-ighness, you decide!"

So my father had to do the deciding. He transferred the mischievous boy to the Odessan Cadet Corps from which he later graduated, joining the cavalry. He earned the St. George's Cross for his feats during the First World War in which he died a hero.

But my father's military career wasn't his only realm of interest.

Being the President of the Russian Academy of Sciences he took part in various scientific projects and the organization of several expeditions, including Admiral Kolchak's polar party.

My parents' family life was remarkably happy and harmonious. My mother never converted to orthodoxy, but being a deeply religious and open-minded person, she didn't object and even supported our devotedly Orthodox father's intention to raise his children within the dogmas of Orthodoxy. From an early age, my brothers used to assist at services and read clerical texts in church. My elder brother Ioann was especially religious and even had his own church choir. In a word, our family life was grounded on the firm foundations of the Orthodox faith.

On his frequent visits to cadet corps and schools, my father watched closely the cadets' behaviour during church services. He could see that even though they made a show of good behaviour and piety, few of them prayed whole-heartedly. "All of you take care of the cleanliness of your body by washing daily," he'd often say to the cadets gathered around him, "but even more so you should take care of the cleanliness of your soul by reading the New Testament daily and finding inspiration in such reading."

My father could never boast a sturdy physique. He had problems with his lungs, kid-neys and heart. He used to say that he had the constant feeling of his heart bleeding. He often went abroad for treatment.

The two winters of 1912 to 1914 my parents spent in Egypt - for the sake of his health but also because both fell in love with it. There they were especially happy because finally they were virtu-ally alone and could enjoy each other's company. These trips to Egypt became, in a way, their be-lated honeymoon.

In the summer of 1914 my father received treatment in Nauheim while my mother, brother George and myself stayed with my maternal grandmother. We'd heard all the vague rumours about an upcoming war, but our father never paid much notice to them: those rumours never stopped in the last pre-war years, waxing and waning, so that finally everybody got used to them. Suddenly Father received a telegram from his younger brother the Grand Duke Dimitri Konstantinovich, informing him of the impending mobilization. Immediately he left for Bad Liebenstein to collect us, in order to go back to Russia.

In those days, the whole of Germany was in a state of militaristic hysteria. They saw Russian spies and motor cars repatriating Russian gold everywhere. Similarly, they mistook our car for one carrying "Russian spies". As we waited for the train at the station, someone in the crowd pointed at my brother and remarked rather impolitely that he could have at least removed the Russian hat (my brother was wearing a Russian sailor's hat with the name *Poteshny* on the ribbon).

The train stopped at the Russian border in Eydtkuhnen. We were ordered to keep our carriage doors and windows open, only allowing us to close them in the children's compartments. I was eight years old at the time, my brother eleven. I remember drinking some milk and eating some black bread. I also remember the sentries standing by the carriage wearing spiked helmets, their dust covers bearing a large number 33. In the morning we were moved to motor cars. Lieutenant Müller who was in charge of our security - and who until then had been quite correct and polite - began addressing my mother as Gnaedike Frau, or Madam - apparently afraid of mentioning her titles.

They kept our father's adjutant Stepyagin and the valets, telling us they'd be able to join us later with the bulk of our luggage. At first they also wanted to detain my father, too, but my mother announced that she would not leave him. They had to telegraph Berlin about it. As far as I can remember, it was the German Empress Augusta Victoria who spoke up for us, insisting they let us through.

We left Eydtkuhnen in two cars: my parents, my brother and I in one and the rest of our party in the other. A soldier with a rifle took the seat next to the chauffeur. They lowered the curtains and told us not to peek out of the windows under penalty of death. My brother and I in our front folding seats tried to peek out all the time which worried our mother a lot.

Suddenly the car jolted to a halt. The doors swung open. Our guard shouted in a frightened voice, "The Cossacks are coming!" They unloaded us literally into the ditch by the side of the highway leading to Verzhbalovo. Neither our father's adjutant nor the valets were there, though. We were told they would join us in twenty minutes. Still, the car never reappeared - neither in twenty minutes, an hour nor in two hours. We kept waiting. Refugees drove past us in their carts. On the other side of the road, a peasant stood in front of his house just opposite us, telling us to leave promptly to escape the Cossacks. I remember myself thinking, "You don't know that we are at one with those Cossacks!"

Finally, a Russian picket appeared - two mounted lancers. They didn't answer our questions. When the main unit arrived, Father's adjutant Prince Shakhovskoy went out to meet them with Father's visit card. The officer stared at the card, uncomprehending. He must have been thinking, how on earth had a Russian Grand Duke ended up in a gutter on the German border on the first day of war! Still, one look at my father (whom he'd seen barely a year ago at the junkers college), told him that it was truly the Grand Duke.

We got to Verzhbalovo station which had been burned down by its own station master, made ourselves comfortable in the Royal lounge and prepared to wait. As it turned out, the Empress Maria Feodorovna's train was waiting in Kowno while she'd chosen to go back to Russia via Denmark and not on to Verzhbalovo as originally planned. Father telephoned Tsarskoe Selo and Pavlovsk. They took us to Kowno in a small train consisting only of the steam engine and a single third-class carriage. Our father was extremely fatigued by everything that had happened, so when my brother and I began running around the carriage playing, we were quickly chastised.

When we finally arrived at Pavlovsk, our

elder brothers were already about to go to the front line.

After a short while, we received the terrible news of brother Oleg having received a mortal wound. Our parents hurried to Vilno where they found him still alive. He died in their arms not twenty minutes after their arrival. Oleg's death was a terrible blow for our father as he was the closest to him of all us children, sharing our father's literary and intellectual interests. This death and everything that had happened during the first days of the war must had sped up his demise.

During the last few years before the war, the health of our dear *papa*, as we used to call him, continued to deteriorate. He was diagnosed with cardiac angina. Its bouts were growing stronger and more frequent. One of them was so powerful we thought his end was near - but still he recovered, to the point where we even decided to visit our favourite estate at Ostashevo near Moscow where we'd laid brother Oleg to rest.

On June 15, 1915 our father sat in bed in his study in Pavlovsk playing solitaire. Our mother was in the bedroom, trying on a summer dress as she packed for our trip to the country. I sat in our father's study on a sofa reading the Russian translation of *The Tale of the Fox*. The room was on the ground floor of our Pavlovsk palace. With three windows, it was long and large. Our father and I were expecting his sister Olga

Konstantinovna, the Queen of the Hellenes.

Aunt Olya, as we called her, used to visit Father at the time to read him some of the Russian classics. Both wanted me present during those readings in order to give me a taste for Russian literature.

We kept waiting, but Aunt Olya was late back from the hospital where she worked as an operating theatre nurse. The valet on duty walked in, reporting that the Queen was busy performing a surgery and that she was expected to be late.

Soon after he left I heard Father gasping for air. I was nine years old at the time and didn't quite grasp the nature of his condition. Still, I'd heard other people discussing his bouts of the disease - enough to realize what was going on. Terrified, I rushed out to fetch Mother, forcing open an incredibly heavy mirrored door leading into her boudoir, then running through the dining room and hallway into her bedroom.

"Papa can't breathe!" I screamed.

Immediately they sent me to the valet to ask him to call the doctor. But the man must have been petrified with shock as he just stood there, uncomprehending, laughing nervously without doing anything.

"Come on, Arakcheev, quick! Papa is very poorly!" I shouted, jumping up and down in desperation, stomping my feet. But it was too late. Everything was already over.

A week later he was buried with full honours. The Imperial family was present. The funeral lasted from two in the afternoon until nine in the evening. I vaguely remember the last church service in Pavlovsk and our train trip via the Imperial line; the serried ranks of cadets and junkers, their colours furled; the St. Peter and Paul's Cathedral, dark and gloomy. I was in one carriage with Her Imperial Majesty, one of the elder Grand Duchesses - I think it was Olga Nikolaevna - and my mother. The heat was unbearable.

We couldn't fathom at the time how merciful Providence had been to him, sending him on to a better world without experiencing any of the horrors of the Revolution that so closely impacted our family.

The first English translation of Prince Gabriel's memoirs, offer a fascinating portrait of the beauty and splendour of the Russian Imperial Court in its twilight years. This is the chronicle of a member of the Romanov dynasty who lived to tell his story.

MEMORIES IN THE MARBLE PALACE
by Prince of the Imperial Blood Gabriel Constantinovich

AVAILABLE FROM AMAZON

Vera was the only Romanov who remembered pre-revolutionary life and her legendary relatives. She was a living embodiment of the best traditions of the House of Romanov, enjoyed great respect and respect in the circles of the Russian emigration.

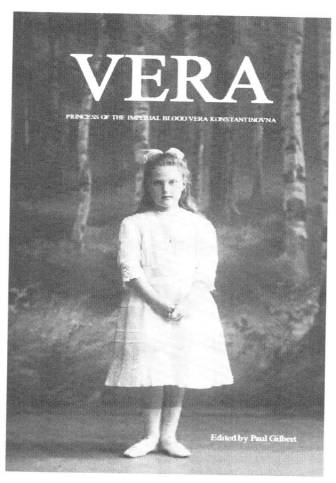

VERA: Princess of the Imperial Blood
Edited by Paul Gilbert

AVAILABLE FROM AMAZON

PAUL GILBERT

Independent Researcher and writer on
the life, reign and era of Nicholas II

"Dedicated to clearing the name of Russia's
much slandered emperor and tsar"

Visit my blog
NICHOLAS II. EMPEROR. TSAR. SAINT.
tsarnicholas.org

Follow me on Facebook
facebook.com/royalrussia

Contact me by e-mail
royalrussia@yahoo.com

Made in United States
Orlando, FL
31 March 2022

16350960R00078